THIS TRUTH
MUST BE TOLD!

THIS TRUTH MUST BE TOLD!

The Untold Journey Through The Eyes Of My Soul

Edna Washington Turner

iUniverse, Inc.
Bloomington

THIS TRUTH MUST BE TOLD!
THE UNTOLD JOURNEY THROUGH THE EYES OF MY SOUL

iUniverse books may be ordered through booksellers or by contacting:

iUniverse
1663 Liberty Drive
Bloomington, IN 47403
www.iuniverse.com
1-800-Authors (1-800-288-4677)

ISBN: 978-1-4620-6644-5 (sc)
ISBN: 978-1-4620-6645-2 (ebk)

Printed in the United States of America

iUniverse rev. date: 12/02/2011

~Contents~

~In Honor of my Husband~

Rev. Phillip E. Turner

Thank the Lord for blessing me with you!

I love you Bae!

~Preface~

This book is many parts of the raw and untold secrets of my life that I've not shared with anyone. These writings come from my heart and are spoken through my voice. Some of these writings may be offensive to those who may recognize themselves through this truth, but through this truth there is freedom.

These writings are not intended to degrade, criticize, or offend anyone, but to allow others to learn from my personal experiences how our actions can affect the lives of others and ourselves for many years.

It has taken over forty years for me to trust in God's promises and step into this place of pain and confusion; knowing I will not leave the same. It is my sincere prayer that this book blesses all who read its contents.

I thank God for giving me the strength to write through the tears, fears, and doubts to express this truth that must be told!

Glory to His Holy Name!

~In Loving Memory~

My Daddy, Marcellus M.C. Washington: The best Father a girl could have been blessed to have. You were a man of honor and never afraid to share your affection towards me. You never degraded or blamed me for my short comings, despite being a strict disciplinarian. You were brutally honest; saying what you meant and meaning what you said. I have tremendous admiration for what you taught me and sacrificed for me. You did one heck of a job Daddy, even when I didn't realize the seed was being planted. You were my one of a kind! I miss you Daddy!

March 31, 1917-February 6, 1984

My Mama, Gertrude Gilford Washington Gray: The best Mother that you knew how to be. You were a strong-willed woman who endured and sacrificed much to provide all that you could for your children. You were big hearted and willing to help anyone, despite many times being taken for granted; even by me. You were a rare breed and despite battling your own personal demons, Mama you loved me the best you knew how. I have much regret because I did not always honor you due to my own pain; I blamed you! Thank the Lord for enabling me in the end to be there when you really needed me, and when I really needed to be there. Rest in peace Mama!

December 29, 1931—August 15, 1999

My Daughter, DeShelle Rena' Branch: I carried you inside me for thirty six weeks and the Lord called you home to be with Him. Although I've cried many tears and my heart has bled from your absence, I strive daily to see you again in our Heavenly home! Mama loves you!

Death date: November 10, 1983

My Sister, Earnestine "Tina" Boone: Although you lived far, you felt so close. You were there for me in times when I really needed you. I was ashamed to reach out, but you made me know it was alright because you were family; my big sis! I miss our talks and receiving your cards of encouragement! I miss them so! Keep smiling down on Royce!

February 26, 1946—January 31, 2009

~Acknowledgements~

Giving all reverence to my Heavenly Father through whom all blessings flow. I thank you Lord for never leaving or forsaking me and providing for me when I didn't even realize where my help was coming from, yet you were right there all the time. Thank you! Thank you! Thank you!

Mr. Delton R. Branch Sr.: You have been a part of my life since I was sixteen years old and demonstrate what unconditional love is, although for so many years I didn't have a clue. Thank you for being supportive and loving me when I didn't love myself. I will always love you and what you represent as a man, father, grandfather and a child of God.

Cedric Washington (Dynita), Delvina Branch, Delton Branch II (Claudia): Mama has made many sacrifices through the years to provide all that I had and could. In some instances, I fell short however not because of lack of effort. I have always and will always desire God's best upon you all, despite my flaws and imperfections. I desire true happiness and freedom for each of you! I love you all from the DEEPEST depth of my heart!

Asiah, Ciyonna, Peyton Washington, Bri'jai Washington, Delton Branch III, Deshawn Branch, and Devin Branch: Granny prays the writings of this book will enable each of you to understand the importance of truth and believing in yourselves when no one else does. Always know that God has all power in His hand and a divine plan for your lives. Follow Him and the possibilities are limitless!

Tommy Washington (Edna), Jerrell Perrin (James), Brenda Robinson (Nathaniel), Wilma Mason, Karl Kincheon Sr. (Cheteral), and Michael Washington (Demarius): May the Lord continue to bless and keep you in His precious care is my continuous prayer. May the truth set us free!

Dorothy Crump, Laura Franklin, Anglyn Denise Tubbs (Rest in Peace Sis), Leroy & Debbie Chaisson & family, Shandolyn Bailey, Annie Gray, Dorothy Barnes, James Gilford, Brenda & Charles Horace, Mr. & Mrs. Charles Connally, Kelly Foreman & Family, Terri Connally, Ellis "Junior" Williams, Lynn Gondesen and Family, Laura Renee' Walker, Mr. & Mrs. Dudley Breaux, and Kenny Boston Sr.: Through the years and tears, you've been by my side. I love you all dearly!

Daddy (Yawkey), K.B., Reggie Red, Buck, Rennie (Rat), Poochie, Ray Ray, Gayland, Bo, Jon Jon, Marcus, Richard, Dre-Day, Georgie, Stebo, Stevie, Freaky, Pauly, Freeman, and Super Dave. Thank you for always being my "4Reals" from the neighborHOOD, standing by my side, and accepting me just as I am! Much love always!!

Timothy Hood, Rae-Shell W. Jenkins, and Maria Martinez. Thanks for the tremendous support through your time, encouragement, and love.

"We Don't Do Drama" Youth Mentoring Program Sponsors, Officers, Members, and Volunteers: Thank the Lord for blessing me with the vision and opening the necessary doors to change lives through His holy and divine word. "Inspiring our youth to inspire through Jesus Christ; Drama-Free!"

My Pastor & Wife, Rev. Robert Sr. & Hilda Eagleton and the entire St. John Baptist Church Family (5th Ward, TX.): Thank you for your continuous prayers, love, and fellowship through my many trials and tribulations knowing that God had already made the way! Thank you for pouring your love on me in abundance! "Building individuals to restore the community back to God"

Pastor & Sis. Emmitt Thompson and the entire Christian Love Missionary Baptist Church Family, Attorney William Jones, Dr. Samuel Pegram, Dr. Marcos Masson, Evangelist Evon Boykins, Rev. & Mrs. Calvin Miller, Rev. Lester Shannon, and Mr. Rick Hill & The

Open Door Mission Family (Houston, TX.). Thank you for your friendship, fellowship, and support through the storms that kept on raging.

The Gifted Educators and Staff of San Jacinto College North & Central campuses: Kaye Winters Moon, Dr. James Semones, Dr. Nancy Carothers, Dr. Deborah Myles, Coach Eric Taylor, Ms. Adanta Ugo, Mr. Sergio Garcia, Mrs. Patricia Petty, Mrs. Stacy Coats, Mr. Ronald Hopkins, Professor Edwin Aiman, and Ms. Beverly Hall. Thank you for your support and commitment as I endured some of the most difficult challenges in my life when I entered college for the first time at forty two years of age. Thank you for pushing me to reach goals I once thought was unreachable!

~Introduction~

As I take this journey into some of the darkest moments of my life, I find it necessary to free myself from the bondage that has kept me imprisoned within. I have fought against traveling this road for it's so much easier to allow it to remain contained inside or so I thought; it has been showing its ugliness outside for longer than I care to remember.

Through this journey I will enter into moments of my past and the honesty of my heart to the freedom through truth that is the release of all situations/circumstances. I will open some scars and express some truths that have been patched up for many, many years and through God's healing power, rejoice in knowing it's out; finally!

I pray that each individual who reads the contents of this book will understand the message and the effect untold secrets can have on the direction of our lives' path. Untold secrets and lies can lead to unexplainable behavior and confusion for generations. I thank God for giving me the strength to move beyond the pain and allowing me to finally recognize the enormous power I have through Him!

This has been shameful, guilt-filled, heart-wrenching feelings I've kept within for over forty years. Yes, over forty years! This has been a journey that through God's grace and mercy has given me the courage and strength to release this pain, shame, confusion, unwelcomed and invasive heartache that are now no longer important enough to contain.

This was and has been my cross to bear for far too many years of my life, and now the time has come for me to let go through the Holy Spirit that now resides within me.

Although, there have been many instances that I've wanted and attempted at getting released from this pain and heartbreak, it wasn't until January 10, 2011 that the Lord said, "It's time." Now, I'm ready to spread my wings and fly like an eagle. Here I go . . .

CHAPTER 1

The Journey Begins

It was August 4, 2009, and as I sat in my living room chair attempting to fall asleep, I was battling against this unknown pain in my chest that had become worse as the hours passed. I had reeled, rocked, shifted positions, and fought against awakening my husband for I did not want another journey to the emergency room. The pain had surpassed what I could no longer disregard and I awoke him and he immediately rushed me off.

As we entered the sliding double doors, the pain was horrific and one that I had not felt before. The emergency room staff immediately proceeded to rush me into the triage unit and began hooking me up to every available piece of equipment they had. They began asking me question after question and seemed to believe I may have been experiencing a heart attack, but the thought of that never crossed my mind! After running test, drawing blood, and zapping most of the energy I had left, the doctor stepped in from behind the drawn curtain and told me, "You have Pericarditis, a swelling and irritation of the pericardium, the thin sac-like membrane that surrounds the heart. The sharp chest pain associated with acute pericarditis occurs when the pericardium rubs against the heart's outer layer." After the medical team explained me, I was treated with a steroid pack and instructed to see a cardiologist. As I was discharged and we drove to the local pharmacy to have the prescription filled, my husband drove me home to remain in bed and allow the medications to take effect.

Two days passed and I was right back at the hospital again, but this time the pain's severity had worsened to an even higher level.

It was deja vu all over again! The doctor ran additional tests and released me again with the same instructions as days prior and I returned home to continue the prescribed regimen. This time after our arrival home, the pain had become so intense that I was crawling on the floor, rolling back and forth on the bed, and suddenly out of nowhere, I told my husband, "Shoot me!" He looked at me with intense passion and said, "Devil, I rebuke you!" He knew that this was not me talking, but the pain had taken its toll and I simply wanted relief, but not that way! He began to pray and brought the other prescribed medications to me and eventually I dozed off. As the months passed and my condition worsened, the many medical professionals still were unable to find a clinical explanation for my symptom's severity. Finally, after another emergency room trip on October 29, 2009, three steroid injections, multiple co-pays, specialist after specialist, I was hospitalized by a well—known Rheumatologist who just couldn't stand the idea that I had suffered all this time, yet still had no answers! He was a fleshly dressed, well groomed, sincere, and compassionate man who cared enough to have me admitted into a local hospital and made arrangements for various health care doctors and specialists to come and examine me, rather than me continuing to go searching for them.

After a four day stay with the pain being somewhat relieved intravenously, there were two diagnoses but still no definite answer as to what was really going on. I was released from the hospital and instructed to see a pain management doctor to assist in trying to get the pain under control. I scheduled my appointment as instructed and met with the physician who believed the pain was coming from my neck. He scheduled me for a trip to the hospital for an outpatient procedure of which he gave me two steroid injections to the second and third vertebrae in my neck. Unfortunately, the results remained the same but now my husband began reflecting back and remembered that a particular specialist' name kept coming up during this almost ten month painfully, indescribable ordeal. He then recommended that I see him, but I was tired of getting no answers and told him, "I will not go to another doctor!" He looked at me and calmly said, "You're going." I felt no need to debate with him for I knew he too had traveled this journey with me and wanted the same thing I wanted; answers and relief. On May 28, 2009, we met God's Chosen

Specialist for the first time and it was a difficult day for me due to the excessive pain!

As he entered the nicely decorated and extremely cold room, he had a smile that shined like none other I had seen, bubbly personality, and soothing bedside manner. He looked over the medical records and asked questions here and there and then proceeded to ask, "May I do a quick diagnostic on you?" At that point I really didn't care one way or the other for I didn't think his outcome would be any different than that of previous doctors and specialists, but thank God I was so wrong! He asked my husband, "Assist your wife to the bed and lay her down." I was in so much pain I couldn't take another step without assistance as he proceeded to walk me to the examination table. He explained cautiously yet confidently, "Your records indicate that there are two possible diagnoses and I will eliminate one of them today." He further explained, "I will step out of the room to get some medications and a syringe." Upon his return, he opened the door and to my amazement, I saw a white ghostly looking shadow that entered and levitated as though it were in flight and hovered in the corner of the room. I didn't say one word because I didn't want him to think I was losing my mind as a result of the pain, but I could feel the presence of the Holy Spirit. He proceeded to inject me in my chest directly below my collar bone, and explained as he went along what I should anticipate. After the injection was entered he then said, "Please lay down for three to four minutes," and once again he left the room. As I continued to lie there, I could feel the pain leaving my body like a magic trick had been performed and I began to cry. My husband asked, "Is it worse, better, or the same?" I couldn't say anything, but I began sobbing like a new born baby because I could feel the pain gradually leaving my body. I screamed, "The pain is gone! It's gone!"

As God's Chosen Specialist reentered, he didn't even ask how I was doing because it was apparent that the injection had worked! He then explained, "You have a rare, often misdiagnosed syndrome; Thoracic Outlet Syndrome; a complex disorder characterized by a constellation of signs and symptoms resulting from the compression of blood vessels and nerves (neurovascular bundle) in the thoracic outlet region where they exit the chest. The *thoracic outlet* is a space located between the thorax (rib cage) and the clavicle (collar bone) which contains major blood vessels (subclavian artery and vein) and nerves (brachial plexus). The thoracic outlet is the area through which nerves and blood vessels travel to and from the arm." After his explanation, he showed us diagraphs and informed us that the injection was a temporary fix, and he needed to place me in thoracic therapy for four weeks. I was hesitant about going but my husband made up my mind for me. On June 25, 2010, after I completed a rigorous four weeks of therapy with a devoted, humble, and compassionate therapist, the pain had progressively worsened. On June 28, 2010, I returned to God's Chosen Specialist with the results in hand from the therapist and he arranged for immediate surgery to remove my first rib. On July 1, 2010, after I had suffered for nine months and three weeks, God positioned me at His appointed time to be informed of what all this process entailed.

This was to become more of a Godly journey than I could have ever imagined and a journey I needed to travel to complete this assignment. God poured into my spirit on January 10, 2011 in the midst of a conversation with my husband that it was time for me to move myself from this pain and speak what must be told! Not simply the pain of the illness, but the pain that had been buried within me for far too long! As my husband pleaded for me to share this heartache, I saw an opening that no longer desired to be shut! It was finally time for me to let go and open up the sufferings of my past and the feelings of my present to be freed from the traps of the enemy. This was a subject that my husband had tried to open up many times during our dating and marriage, yet each time I said, "I don't want to talk about it; it's too painful and shameful!" He had always been supportive and calmly said, "It won't get better until you let it go." My mind did as it had done so many times before; wonder! Why was it so important for him to know these unwelcomed visitors inside of me, for they belonged to me, and I didn't want anyone to know of this darkness, shame, guilt, and humiliation! Most of my life the only words that I had heard were derogatory, and I believed them for many years. I was surrounded by many who said they wanted the best for me, yet their actions demonstrated the complete opposite. Although, I could remember some of the positive people in my surroundings, I still struggled with many of the memories that were lost in the depth of my mind for reasons that only God knew. I had compromised myself for others for so long and my decisions now were being driven by a greater power than me; God's power! This power had driven me to stop trying to please others for it was causing me to remain in bondage, but instead speak truth in order to be set free!

We often discussed my inability and unwillingness to talk about these issues and I used every excuse in the book except the truth! As I began to question myself I asked, "Do you really want to open this Pandora's Box and are you prepared to deal with what could come from this inner child that had kept quiet for so long?" At this point, it really didn't matter for the time had come for me to face my demons and stop pretending they weren't there. As I took a deep breath, the words began pouring out of my mouth like water falling from a waterfall. I started to speak of how my innocence was stolen from me at five years old by a thieving sexual predator! This first predator was a member of the family and although he wasn't my Mama's brother we referred to him as Uncle. Who could have known that this freshly pressed overall clothed, short, bald, old, and musty cologne wearing man was the disguise of the Beast? Who knew I wouldn't say a word and the many tears that were there and yet to follow? As the Beast would regularly come to our old wood framed home and walk up the front stairs unto our porch, he was welcomed in by me after hearing the knock at the door. My memory was faded as to if he started violating me immediately upon entering, or if he manipulated my innocent mind with his words of comfort. He would proceed indoors with his cigar in tow, huge, evil grin, along with the horrific memories that would be left behind each time. He would enter and begin kissing my lips, then sticking his disgusting tongue in my mouth! Cigars; the awful lingering stench and taste that never left my mind! He then started by sticking his finger up my tiny vagina over and over again, despite my attempts to pull away from him and the enormous pain. He would ask, "Do you like it, or does that feel good to you?" Confusion filled my mind for how could I have liked something that was causing me so much indescribable and undesirable pain?

This pain swept through my body along with the awful shame, filthiness, and guilt that I didn't dare share with anyone! I stepped out of myself and closed my eyes in these moments, but the aching, piercing pain was just too much to make a difference. He came and went as though I were a rag doll and even had the gall to smile each time with his evilness as he exited the door. I always wondered where my Mama and siblings were during these moments of filth and despair. Why had he chosen me and how many others possibly in or outside of my family had been victimized by this monster? We knew that Mama made daily visits to the Lone Joint for her daily Smirnoff ritual to deal with her own pain, but how could she not have known? He came for more years than I could remember, but the pain became a constant companion of the wounds that had cut me so deep! Shortly after, Sneaky Eyes showed up with his bucked eyes, deep voice, sailor's tongue, mouth drooling like a dog, and utter disgust filled my entire body! Despite my youthful years, I could feel what he was seeking but who could I talk to about these feelings? I could feel this because I was in familiar territory and the thought made me feel overwhelmingly leery and uncomfortable. His stares were as those of the Beast and when he stopped by, I watched him enter our small kitchen and I raced to hide behind the bunk beds up against the wall. When I saw his feet coming closer and closer my heart raced faster and faster, but thank God, he didn't find me this time! When I slept I would see him in my dreams, but I couldn't understand. What kind of persons were these to prey on an innocent, defenseless child?

Although, we were often home alone to do things for ourselves, it was not something that made us feel neglected. Mama worked hard and did all that she could to provide for her children and even though we were considered to be poor socially, I didn't feel that way. Other than the Scary Little Boy's adamant refusal to go to the corner store for minor purchases with food stamps, I would go with enthusiasm because those books of paper were providing us with a daily meal. I was even allowed to get snacks since I was willing to take the trips to the store, although secretly I wanted to go to ensure that I wasn't home if the Beast or Sneaky Eyes decided to stop by unannounced as they always had. I would even make the trips longer, despite the store being on the corner from our house. As this abuse continued, my memories had only enabled me to remember bits and pieces of the depth of this pain. The pain ran so deep that I knew it was far more than my youthful mind could handle. However, despite all the pain there were moments when happier memories creped their way into my life.

These moments came from inside the walls of the Landmark in the Hill Country. It was a large, historical, and predominately white school with many classrooms to accommodate all its students. The hallways were full of teachers greeting each student as we entered, and once inside it was as though time stood still. Not much for concern here for I was surrounded by love from both teachers and classmates who cared and went the extra mile for a young colored girl in the seventies. This was a time and place that if there was going to be disarray in my life, I would have thought it to come from here, instead this place provided a safe haven. My pain would go away to once again return when I was homeward bound taking public transportation from school to who knew what each day. Often times, Mama had a boyfriend who took Scary Little Boy and me to school, and on some weekends he took us on road trips that we enjoyed, despite having to pull to the side of the road on our return because he had too much to drink. We would use these opportunities to take small weeds and leaves from the side of the highway to rub against his nose and face, and we watched him swat at them as though they were bugs. We created this entertainment to pass the time without the boredom of the hours that would pass before we would begin to continue our journey home.

As I continued, I just couldn't remember the frequency between the abuse and happy memories of my childhood and adolescent years. There had to be more than just pain and a handful of happy memories to remember for me, yet I still needed and wanted answers! This was absolute madness to try to explain when it was something that I couldn't even understand myself. Sometimes, I thought I wanted to know and then other times, I didn't ever want to know! I feared that it would only rehash the pain that I had battled with my entire life to make go away! This pain had been kept buried deep inside of me and as I took another deep breath, I found my mind racing yet again. I was trapped within and wanted a way out of this torment, but questioned if I had done something wrong to deserve it. Many times as the Scary Little Boy and I arrived home, we would receive a message that Mama had over done it with her addiction and off we would have to go to bring her home. This was a weekly and sometimes daily routine she had of attempting to drown her sorrows, regrets, and pains in the bottle of her preference.

As we would begin our trek home from her watering hole, the Scary Little Boy and I would carefully hold her tight on each side to prevent us from falling. Once we made it back home, we undressed her, and helped her into bed to sleep off the days' events that sometimes would last for days. What had we done to create this pain that was within her and why had we been left to take on this tremendous responsibility? Mrs. Good Intentions lived in a nearby city and drove down with Mr. Mellow Fellow for holidays; Easter and Christmas mostly, although it could have been more often. For Easter, Mrs. Good Intentions dressed me in lavish dresses, ruffle socks and occasionally a bonnet that I would be told to wear. I detested the thought of these occasions, but I wouldn't even consider having told her that! She often came bearing gifts and made me feel even smaller and undeserving by her verbal attacks about having to do it! Was it my fault she was so angry and behaved as though she hated me? Why had she continued doing these deeds for so many years knowing it was causing her so much grief? She would take us in the car with her and say things like, "Someone stinks or did you brush your teeth?" She would be so degrading and the words stuck like thorns in my flesh, yet sometimes she appeared to find pleasure in these methods of humiliating me and the Scary Little Boy.

She looked at me with such disgust and I wondered many times was it me she saw or a reflection of herself? Then the time came that we were told Mama was going to be placed in the State hospital for her alcoholism. This was something that drove me into further confusion, although I recognized that she had a problem with drinking, she woke up, functioned, and went to work every day! We were sent to Mrs. Long Distance who was a soft spoken, pack rat, with a passive personality with everyone except us. Things became even worse and before the end of our unwelcomed visit, Scary Little Boy grew courage from the many undeserved spankings we received daily, and a ride was dispatched to pick us up to return to the Lone Star state immediately!

CHAPTER 2

Moving to the Big City

A few years passed and I was entering the sixth grade, the Beast and Sneaky Eyes weren't coming around anymore, but why should they at this point when the damage had already been done! We were preparing to move into a house that Mama qualified for through the Public Welfare System's housing program. We moved from our old neighborhood in our old wood framed house, to a lovely three bedroom brick house with a fenced backyard, and a creek that ran behind it. Things were beginning to look new in more ways than one, as we began meeting new friends and attending a new school. I was yet again attending another incredible school that sat at the top of a large mountain surrounded by magnificently beautiful trees as far as my eyes could see. The landscape was breath-taking as I looked down from the mountaintop and I was putting forth every effort adjusting to being in a less dramatic environment. Yes, Mama was still drinking, but the Lone Joint was too far for her to walk and we didn't have a car. It worked for me because the monsters weren't coming around and I was trying to remove the horrific memories of their gruesome visits and the guilt of keeping silent. I began hanging with children my own age, although there was a handsome, clean shaven, soft spoken mid-twenties gentleman in our midst, but I had no feelings outside of a simple crush for him, and he surprisingly made no advances towards me. We enjoyed all the time of adventure, sliding down the hill on cardboard boxes to the bottom, swinging from ropes that we tied to the trees that filled the creek on each side, and fishing the creek for golf balls that would wash up from the nearby golf course.

I was taking adventures with our friends with no fears and daring anyone to touch me or the Scary Little Boy. Although, we both were little daredevils, Scary Little Boy was not a fighter, but it seemed that was all I wanted to do! He was known for getting me in trouble, but each time I followed him to various destinations just to be in his company. He was a character and made me and others laugh with his antics. He could eat off the land like someone stranded on a deserted island and kept his BB gun close in the event his stomach rumbled while we were out playing. Although, no matter how hungry I was, I had no desire to eat what he was hunting or cooking! These were some good times, yet unfortunately short lived. My battle within was roaring and the old memories were resurfacing and I did not know how to let go of the pain from the past. I wanted that old stuff behind me, but instead focused on memories that just would not go away! The Scary Little Boy had memories also, but they were far different from that of my own. How could that be the case when we shared the same household? How could he remember things that were so different from those things that I remembered? My new friends were having birthday parties and extending invitations that now created more confusion within me because I couldn't remember having any birthday parties of my own.

As I fought my way through, it was back to playing and trying to leave the pain and confusion behind me, and out of nowhere along came this short framed, big car driving, bald headed, cigar toting man at our door seeking Mama's company; the remembrance of a familiar face. The Smooth Talker wasted no time and begun to whisper sweet nothings into Mama's ears and once again things were about to change. Every question imaginable was going through my mind, yet before long his intentions were made very clear. Little time passed before we were told, "We're moving to the big city!" I had been there to visit family, but had not considered the possibility of relocation. Why would she consider leaving the lovely monster free house, my friends, my school, and my teachers? It became apparent quickly that this was something that was going to happen and anything I could say to oppose it would be done in vain!

The day arrived and it was time to move from what we had known to the unknown although he had given us a description of what to expect. The Smooth Talker claimed to be taking us to a better life where there was a big house, swimming pool in the backyard, and many other amenities that we were looking forward to experiencing. I began to think maybe this wouldn't be so bad and could work out in our favor, yet the butterflies continued rumbling in my gut. He continued describing all the benefits we would have and the excitement sat in as we traveled and nodded off to sleep in the backseat. After a little over a couple of hours, the Smooth Talker awoke us and we immediately jumped up to look around and the questions began at the same rate of speed. Where was the big house that he had told us about? Where was the swimming pool and all the other amenities that he continually talked about? As we hesitantly stepped out of the car, we walked up the cement stairs, entered the doorway, and began to walk through the tiny, wood framed house. The living and dining rooms occupied the same space, and the small kitchen sat at the back of the house. The other three rooms were to the right of the entry, and both bedrooms were divided by the bathroom. The back door in the kitchen that entered into the backyard was covered by a refrigerator, therefore we had to go through the front door and walk around the house to the back. It was a large yard that had not been landscaped or maintained, with a plastic above ground swimming pool that had standing water which appeared to have been there for years! I was floored and couldn't believe what I was seeing and because of his deception, we had taken a huge step backwards!

My mind raced with malicious and angry thoughts because why had he told us such lies, and why had she relocated us to move with a stranger expecting a fairy tale ending? Reality had hit like a ton of bricks and all the excitement blew out of me like a balloon! She was smiling as though she were excited, but I could see she was just as shocked as we were, however she had mastered the technique of giving a false appearance. Through the years, she had to in order to protect herself or so she thought? I could read her like a book because I was more like her than I wanted to admit. I guess it really was true, "The apple doesn't fall too far from the tree." Who was I to talk about her failure to show her real emotions, when I had not been real myself? It was so much easier to point the finger at her because then I wouldn't have to look at myself! I was a teenager and knew right from wrong, but chose to pick up some habits that were becoming progressively worse and continuing to use excuses. I became disrespectful towards her and him, even going so far as cursing them as I complained of my agitation. In addition, I did as much as I could to show them how much I resented their decision to relocate us. My foolish mind was telling me so much that I knew was not the right thing, but I did it anyway! Why wasn't I just appreciative and go with the flow instead of focusing on the negative? In my mind, this dream land had now turned into dread land and I couldn't see past my own selfishness and resentment.

The Young One was with Mrs. Good Intentions and Mr. Mellow Fellow, as he had been for a while and I felt like he was the blessed one being with them, but discovered that was again something else I knew nothing about. At least we stayed with Mama and that should have counted for something; right? What difference did I really believe our staying made, for it was not as though we had another option. As I was trying to adjust to having to give up my own room for the first time in my life, to being in his smaller house, I constantly reminded myself that at least I wasn't out on the streets, but then Mama was telling us they were planning to get married! What had he said or done for her to make that decision in such a short time? He had been deceitful to her from the beginning and she was still legally married to Daddy and he knew! Although, Mama and Daddy had been separated for years, they shared a civil relationship with one another. Sound familiar? He recommended that she not remarry to ensure that the social security benefits she received from him would not stop. He didn't care about the Smooth Talker one way or the other, but he wanted the best for Mama and his children. Daddy raised us all as his biological children, despite that not being the case and did not play favoritism! Mama listened at Daddy's concerns and proceeded to divorce him and married the Smooth Talker regardless of our disapproval.

They decided to have a small, intimate wedding with family and a few friends at his house in the yard. When I addressed Mama about not knowing much about this man, she simply said, "We dated in our younger years." I said nothing in reply, but my mind was going one hundred miles per hour with what that past fact had to do with that present hour, or was that the reason she married him? Mama was a glowing bride, but I still protested and became even angrier with them! I couldn't help but to wonder if she thought he had returned like a knight in shining armor, yet felt this was no fairy tale! The wedding ceremony was performed and the marriage started off just as the brief courtship had; on the wrong foot. Mama's personality was much too strong for this little, old man and she showed him no respect and therefore, neither did we! They were married, playing the part, but I could see through the fussing, cursing, and bashing that he had not lived up to her expectation, yet they continued to go through the motions and so did we.

Another year slowly passed and Mama worked and held on for the ride. I had met new friends and was spending most of my time outside the house to prevent having to deal with the daily soap opera going on inside the house. A few months later, Mama was preparing to go to the Hill Country for the funeral service of one of our relatives, and decided she would leave us behind with him. The Scary Little Boy and I were left alone with the Smooth Talker for the first time and the butterflies in my stomach were dancing, although I had not felt them since we initially arrived. As I awoke the morning she left, I did my usual minor cleaning and went outside to play, but then returned home because of the teasing of my hair that would grow down the back of my neck which was embarrassing to me. I expressed my agitation out loud to myself and the Smooth Talker over heard me and volunteered to give me an edge-up. I had seen him shave himself many times and accepted his offer. As he motioned for me, I sat on the floor in the bedroom he shared with my Mama as he sat on the edge of the bed. He started to edge my neck moving my head from side to side and attempted to control his burning urge within, but instead it controlled him. He proceeded to reach over my shoulders, placed his left hand on my left breast and his right hand on my right breast and then squeezed them with a disgusting breath of pleasure coming from his vocals. As I jumped to my feet and began screaming vulgarities in a way that would shame a ship fully loaded with sailors, I quickly ran out the front door. I ran to a nearby friend's house to try to wrap my head around why this was happening to me yet again! What had I done this time and what was it about me that seemed to draw these monsters? My heart felt as though I had done nothing, but my mind was thinking something totally opposite.

I was angry, tired, and disgusted, yet I felt so helpless! After I returned home, I decided I would allow this matter to be dealt with once Mama returned home and she would torment him far once than I could had. As we prepared for bed later, I was awakened by the Smooth Talker climbing over me to get to the other side of the bed against the wall. I once again jumped up out of the bed and began to run into the living room where Scary Little Boy was sleeping, yet I didn't remember if I awoke him or not, but I didn't return to the bedroom, and the Smooth Talker did not come into the living room! I didn't know what to do because now the monster wasn't stopping by unexpectedly, but he lived with me! I wanted to do something, but since I didn't know, I decided I was going to stick with my initial decision to tell Mama, because I was not going to allow another predator to get away with abusing me or attempting to do so. Anyway, I really thought her torment would be far worse that anything I could have done or said. Had the butterflies in my gut been the warning that I had felt from the moment he entered my space? Had the butterflies in my stomach identified that demon from the start? As I tried to ignore the feelings of disgust, anger, fear, and frustration, the memories from the previous abuse kept stabbing deeper and deeper, and finally the longest two days had finally arrived for Mama's return home.

I knew she would take care of him because this time I was telling her what he had done! I anxiously awaited her arrival and as she entered I immediately started screaming to the top of my lungs, "Mama, he tried to do something to me, touched my breasts, and even climbed in the bed with me while I was sleeping!" She looked at me as though she were looking right through me and said, "Girl, you just can't stand to see me happy!" I could not believe what I heard and all the air was popped out of me once again! She could not be serious about this admission that I dare not say if it were not true! Did she really believe that I didn't want to see her happy and I was trying to create havoc to ensure it? Again, the memories were flooding in like a dam bursting to be lowered and the horrific past resurfaced and the entire basis of our relationship had changed for the far worse! I was being accused of lying and that could not be further from the truth, yet it meant absolutely nothing! Although I was disappointed by her response, a part of me regretfully anticipated that she would not defend me, but instead I would be treated as though I were the enemy; I was right! I was no longer the child that she birth into this world, but instead the one that didn't want to see her happy and only wanted to sabotage her marriage or whatever it was!

My destructive behavior escalated and I was acting out and threatened to tell Daddy to validate to Mama that I was telling the truth. She knew my accusations were valid; otherwise she would not have pleaded with me to keep quiet! She knew that if I told Daddy he would beat me down if I were lying because he always told us, "He hated a liar and a thief!" She knew if I were willing to tell him, it was true, but she never admitted it to me or anyone else for that matter. I understood why they were fearful of that revelation being told to Daddy, because they knew he would kill him, and that thought was the deciding factor as to why I didn't! He would have stopped this many years earlier had I said something, but how could I dare have my Daddy go to prison because of me? As we continued going through the motions, we rode together on another trip to the Hill Country and as we drove up the highway, Mama was fussing and cursing without reason. She was upset with the Smooth Talker, but was taking it out on us; especially me! After we returned to the Big City, Mama informed us, "We're leaving!" The confusion in my mind had become more regular than I ever could have imagined or desired. We were leaving over a petty argument she had with him, but not for his attempted sexual assaults of me; her daughter! Although I had mixed emotions from all that had transpired, I didn't know what to think in regards to her unexpected decision. However, since when did what I think matter anyway because she was strong willed and did exactly what she wanted to do! If only she would have used that same strength and left him for what he attempted to do to me!

It was off to the hood we went and this time Mama's rental house was being paid for by the domestic work she had done for as long as I could remember. She worked five days a week and sometimes six causing her to travel many miles from our residence, but she enjoyed what she did. She received what I thought were pitiful trinkets and hand me downs from the resident's homes that she cleaned; not to mention the many children she raised. Although, she did have those few who recognized her work ethic, loyalty, and dedication to them and considered her a part of their families and treated her with the respect she deserved. Even the regulars on the local Metropolitan bus service would save her a seat to ensure they had front row seats as she entertained them with her tales regarding us and whatever else she wanted to talk about; which was pretty much everything. She was like their morning coffee and I remembered how often she would talk about many of their life's issues and once rode with her and had an opportunity to witness how much they knew regarding mine. All eyes were on me once I was identified by name and I couldn't help but to wonder, what all had she told these strangers about me? Why did I even care because it wasn't as though she was telling them something that she had not already told me to my face!

CHAPTER 3

I Thought I Knew it All

Once again this madness had squirmed its way to the top regardless of my efforts to keep it contained. I didn't want family, friends, or strangers to know anything about me outside of the façade that I had portrayed. As far as I was concerned it was none of their business because it was my life and my choice. Yet, the nerve of me to say it wasn't anyone's business when my actions were affecting others around me. I shut the door on anyone's concerns and continued going through the motions of life and again another sexual predator had wormed his way into my space. The Coach was a smooth talking, muscular built, deceitful, and phony predator that lived in the neighborhood and started a teenage girls softball team. It started off being so much fun and I loved playing because I was such a tomboy. He would spend lots of time training me one on one on how to hold the bat, watch the ball after it was pitched, and showed me attention that I otherwise lacked. Before I knew it, I had stepped into another predator's pathway and he gradually manipulated me into trips to the motel at the ripe young age of thirteen years old. This experience by no means was a pleasurable one to any degree, yet I pretended it was the best thing that had ever happened to me. My innocence and trust was taken away again and this time I couldn't blame anyone other than myself! Was the yearning inside of me so great that I would continue to be treated with such disrespect and indignity? He was much older than me and it wasn't long before he had made his rounds to the next girl on the team, until possibly going through each of us. I didn't ask and no one said a mumbling word one way or the other. I started to think about the many times the crippling words from my Mama's mouth rang in my ears and buried themselves in my heart. She often said, "You'll never be shit with your sorry ass!" Not to mention how she would constantly call me, "Sorry bitches and whores!" Was she able to see something in me that I didn't know was there through some of her very own pain, or had she cursed me with her words because she believed them to be true?

Another year passed and I had become even worse, hanging with my road dog, and walking the streets all times of the day and night, and behaving as though I was grown. My Road Dog was like the big sister I never really had, outspoken, a fighter with the drop of a hat, and street smart. She was protective of me and wouldn't allow anyone to take advantage of me in her presence. She was popular in our hood and many people knew her and had their own negative opinions regarding her, but we hit it off immediately! She introduced me to a lifestyle where I didn't belong, but was accepted and therefore held on for the ride. I was doing what I wanted because that's exactly what Mama had done and made it easier for me to justify my recklessness. She had once again allowed the Smooth Talker to worm himself back into our lives! How on earth could this be with all that we had been through with him? I thought she deserved so much more than the same tired and vicious never-ending cycle that she was in and couldn't understand why she didn't! Even after his return, when she was angry with him she would have the Scary Little Boy and I throw all of his clothes out in the front yard, and we would run with excitement back and forth with hands full of clothes, tossing them up in the air and watching them fall to the ground. Yet again, another year had passed and I was living a life far beyond that of a fifteen year old child. My Road Dog had even gone as far as to get me a job at a neighborhood hole in the wall as a waitress. The joint's owner upon hiring me, despite knowing my age told me, "If the police come in, just say you're my daughter." Another woman who didn't care, but instead used me for her personal gain, but why did I care when no one else seemed to? The work was easy enough, not to mention my own money and I was all personality and got along well with the crowd for I had mastered the façade to the fullest.

I was working and partying every weekend, and sometimes in the middle of the week leaving with money in tow of which made me feel very pleased. Why doesn't this root of all evil make my pain go away if for only a moment? I should have been home where a child my age should have been. I would instead go to work and entered the weekly dance contest and the prize would always be a fifth of whatever the popular alcoholic beverage was and I danced my heart out to ensure that everyone drank on me, despite not being much of a drinker myself. It was entertainment, yet emptiness filled me each night as I would leave to go home. I still lived in my Mama's house but she said nothing outside of the few times she would lock me out due to my late arrival home. I began seeing older men, many who were married, because I didn't want a man who wanted to hang around me all the time. I just wanted him around when I wanted him around! I didn't know their wives or wanted to know them either for I knew what I was doing was wrong, and would not betray a woman by looking her in the face and sleeping with her husband behind her back.

I felt that as long as I didn't know her, and she didn't know me; there was no harm in what I was doing. What a fool I was! Did I think that a healthy relationship was impossible to find or had I chosen this path because of past issues? It didn't matter that I thought I was grown and beyond my years, I was a child! I was so unhappy but didn't understand why and it became so bad that I didn't care that I was headed for self-destruction! I was working in this joint, staying out until all times of the night, and my life had spiraled out of control! I was reliving a life that had already been lived by my Mama yet, I was searching for something out there that I would not find. I was catching the eyes of men and they were telling me, "I'm beautiful, have a wonderful personality, and a gorgeous smile!" These were comments that had not often been heard by me in my young but fast lived life. Considering the selection, why did I choose the married ones and why had they allowed themselves to be chosen? These relationships or whatever they were called were not healthy ones and I had witnessed the results with friends, yet I still continued to do what I was allowed to do. I was spending time with two different married men and neither knew until their crossed paths while we were out partying. Despite knowing that I was out of control, sadly I didn't even know if I wanted out. I was picking and choosing, going from one disastrous relationship to another while looking for someone to blame, when the real disaster was me!

I was mishandling them and they just thought it was my immaturity, but it was just another result of my recklessness. I was living the disastrous life that I had been told I would and felt that I deserved. I didn't have a clue what I was doing and questioned what happened to the dream of the white picket fence, nursing school, and making my parents proud. I thought that I controlled the conditions of these relationships, but those were foolish and immature thoughts for I had no control! The predators were in my head and I couldn't make them go away no matter how hard I tried, and so weekend after weekend I was waiting tables, dancing, attempting to drink, and partying to make the pain inside go away! I was hanging out with the so-called thugs and hoodlums, joint hopping, hustling, smoking marijuana, being promiscuous and so much more. I continued to settle for less than I deserved and continued beating myself up over issues of the past. I was literally trying to do what I felt so many others had done; destroy myself! I knew better and had no excuses but instead made the choices that I really believed were beneficial to me. I continued going to high school and was in my junior year, but before long I was skipping class more often to go layup with the Donor Dad. The Donor Dad was introduced to me by an acquaintance in the hood and I started to develop loving feelings for him. He was handsome, tall, and had a deceitfully charming attitude. The more I saw him, the more I wanted to see him and Mama allowed me to, although, she was unaware that I had been secretly seeing him for months before they were formally introduced. In addition, I had not told her he was married or the many times he had hit me in my face, stomach, and threatened me with his guns.

I had not told anyone of this monster whom I had fallen madly in love with, for how could I be? Why had I accepted this abuse when I would beat a man down for reasons far less than these? By that time, he prepared to move into his own apartment and I foolishly moved in with him at his request, although I was still far from being committed to him, despite my feeling towards. Shortly after moving, I returned to our apartment from an escapade with the Pool Shark who was married, good looking, and charming. He had a good job and spoiled me by catering to my every whim, not to mention his expertise in my favorite game; billiards. Despite showing a little jealousy from time to time, he was very protective of me and often expressed his love for me. As I entered the apartment, I was shortly followed by the Donor Dad and his own escapade partner in tow straight to our bedroom. They walked directly passed me as though I was invisible as the sounds of lust and the scent of sex roamed down the hallway towards my ears and nostrils. Yes, he was having sex with this woman while I sat in the living room watching television in complete disbelief! I began to cry as though it was alright for me, but the nerve of him was heartbreaking. I was behaving as though I was completely innocent of what I had just returned from doing myself. I called the Pool Shark to come and pick me up and quicker than quick he showed up ready to confront the Donor Dad, but I stopped him because what difference would that have made? As we departed, he drove me back to Mama's house where I should have been all along. It wasn't as though the Pool Shark could take me home to his wife, and once again I was right back where I started from, yet this experience had taught me nothing!

Shortly thereafter, the Donor Dad returned to Mama's and smooth talked his way back into my life and bed. Umm, sound familiar? I was then persuaded to return to school and finish to receive my diploma, but began feeling sick every day, causing me to leave class for regular trips to the ladies room to face the porcelain throne. Weeks later, I went home and told Mama about these episodes and she said, "You need to go to the doctor and see what is wrong with you." We had no insurance but plenty of free clinics and off I went to be told, "Sweetie, you're pregnant." I didn't know how to react or feel for this was surprising and unexpected. I returned home and told Mama and the Donor Dad about the news of becoming a teenage parent. Mama was supportive and even took trips with me to my doctor's visits on occasion, but shortly thereafter Donor Dad was gone! Amazingly, it didn't even catch me by surprise for he had already walked out on one child with his wife so what made this child any different? I didn't really know how I felt about him leaving, but I did know I wanted to have a healthy baby to love and who loved me. As my pregnancy entered its fourth month, I was off to the neighborhood joint to keep my mind off the confusion of him up and leaving. Although, when he was there it was for reasons that differed from those of my own, so why in the world was I trying to keep my mind occupied because he was gone?

As my Road Dog and I continued doing our usual hanging out, that was the time I was introduced to her longtime friend, Mr. Good Guy who eventually became my first husband. We had partied together that night and after the joint closed at two in the morning we were preparing to leave and he asked, "Would you like to go out to eat?" Of course I immediately said, "Yes!" It wasn't as though I was ready to go home, despite being out into the early morning hours. He was such a gentleman, soft spoken, humble spirited, and giving. Mr. Good Guy was a keeper, but there was one problem; he was in love with another woman and our conversation showed two things to me. First, she was using him in the same manner I had used men and secondly, he loved her despite her deceit and infidelity. As the months passed, my pregnancy was progressing nicely and I was taking the bus back and forth to the clinic for my prenatal care. I was still battling with attending school, living at home, and the morning sickness that lasted all day. I decided it was time for me to go home to tell Mama, "I'm not going back to school!" She angrily responded, "It's your life!" She had her own issues to deal with and since I was acting grown she allowed me to take on adult responsibilities and decisions.

Another seven months passed, and out of nowhere the Donor Dad returned and weaseled his way into my life again, as though he had never gone away. I had mixed feelings regarding his return and questioned as to why he was back and where he had been. However, before any questions could be asked, he was welcomed back in with open arms. What was going on with me and why would I allow him back after being gone for so long? I had began to hang out with Mr. Good Guy, yet that came to a screeching halt upon the Donor Dad's return, although Mr. Good Guy was still fighting for the same thing as me; a dead end relationship! As we welcomed the Donor Dad back, a couple of months later I was awakened by tremendous pain and the gushing of water coming from between my legs. I was puzzled as to what was happening for I had been to the clinic, but it was apparent, I had asked all the wrong questions in regards to what I should expect. I was already a week passed the due date the doctor had given me, but still clueless as to what was going on. As Mama raced to the phone to call for the ambulance, the Young One ran to the end of the block to ensure that the ambulance didn't pass our street. As they took me in the ambulance, I looked up in the headliner and there was a yellow smiling face sticker that I found amusing considering I was in extreme pain! In August 1982, we arrived at the hospital and as they began rolling me down the hallway, this little one wasn't waiting to enter this world. The paramedics proceeded to deliver my first bundle of joy in the hallway of the local county maternity hospital with people passing and looking as though they were attending a three ring circus.

CHAPTER 4

The Donor Dad and His Visitor

D espite the many questions, my handsome child and I arrived home and everything seemed to come natural for me. I loved this child and wanted the best for him and wanted nothing more than to protect him from any hurt, harm or danger of any degree! His Donor Dad had come around more occasionally, more often, and then it appeared he possibly would be hanging around for the long haul. Three weeks passed and I wanted to get back out and hang with the crew although my Mama continued to say, "You need to stay in this house for another three weeks girl!" I was so ready to get out and see what I had missed and what was going on. I knew these thoughts were complete madness because I had not even allowed my body to heal from the delivery of my child, but out to run the streets I went! As Donor Dad arrived to pick me up, we headed to a joint in the hood that I often frequented. As we entered to the sounds of loud music and neighborhood friends and foes, we walked in being greeting by most with every step we took. I loved being out again and soon one of my favorite tunes hit the DJ's turntable and off for the dance floor I went as I watched someone call the Donor Dad outside. As he stepped outside, almost immediate gunfire overpowered the sound of music I danced to, and I raced to the door without thought to find the Donor Dad lying in a puddle of his own blood. He was severely injured and the joint's owner called for the ambulance and he was loaded in and we headed to the local trauma hospital. They were telling me, "We can't work on him without permission from a family member," so I said, "I'm his wife just save his life!" I wasn't his wife, but I didn't want him to die! As I sat in the waiting area alone wondering who to call, I anxiously awaited a report of his condition; the news was not good. They told me, "Contact his other family members for he may not live through the night." I was thinking, "You can't be serious and this can't be happening!"

I also struggled with guilt from being the person who initiated wanting to go out in the first place and felt that if we weren't there, he would not have been shot. Almost as quickly as I contacted his family, the word began to spread like a wildfire and many had already started spreading the rumor that he had died! Everyone wanted to know what had happened and I only knew that someone had shot him! As he fought for his life, days turned into weeks, weeks into months, and he gradually improved but then they were saying, "He has developed gangrene in his right toes and it was spreading therefore, he needed to consider allowing them to amputate his right leg."At this point he wanted to live and despite not wanting to lose his leg, he gave his signed consent for them to remove it. He had difficult days ahead but I was committed to being there for him and taking care of him for the sake of our child and my guilt. I traveled to the hospital daily and wouldn't allow anything or anyone interfere with what I had to do to care for him. He then developed an infection and had to be placed in isolation and many days I found him down and discouraged, but I continued doing all that I could to raise his spirit. As I continued with my regular visits and his condition improved although he remained in the intensive care unit, he was adjusting to life without his leg but also struggling with it at the same time.

He had mood swings like a menopausal woman, but I would stay there to ride it out just as my guilt had obligated me to. One day as I was running a little behind schedule for the short fifteen minute intensive care unit visit that was allowed, as I stood waiting to enter, I noticed a strange woman staring at me. I didn't have any idea as to who she was and therefore paid her stares little to no attention. As I prepared to enter for my daily visit, the nurse said, "He has had his visitor for this visitation hour." I stepped back and questioned who this visitor was considering I was standing right there waiting. How did someone get in before me and this was my regular routine? I patiently waited outside to see who this visitor was but began to question if I really wanted to know. I was not one to make a scene publically and only fought when I was provoked or protecting someone I loved. I was concerned this visitor might provoke me and just as I turned to walk away, this strange, young, light skinned, and dark haired woman walked up to me. It was the same woman that was giving me the staring eyes as we waited outside of the intensive care unit's entrance. She had a huge envelope in her hand and proceeded to take out a picture of this beautiful baby and said to me, "This is his daughter." She then told me that she should have been born in the same month as my child but was premature and arrived two months earlier. I responded saying, "Are you telling me we were pregnant at the same time?" She answered, "Yes!" She knew all about me but I was completely blind regarding her and furious, but contained my anger because I needed clarity from the Donor Dad!

She told me, "He has been with me the months he was away from you." I couldn't believe what I was hearing but why would she lie about something like that, or did she have something to gain from this revelation? After I regained my composure from what I was hearing and brought our conversation to a close, I waited for the next visitation hour to arrive. I couldn't wait to confront him with what I was told earlier and after I entered his isolated room I began my interrogation. I asked question after question as he began to become evasive until he finally admitted it was his child! He showed no remorse or guilt regarding this newly discovered information to me! He simply said, "It's true." I questioned him yet again and he arrogantly answered those questions he desired, and those that he didn't, I received no answers. I left his room to later return as though I were on a winding road and continued caring for him and supporting him in spite of the surprisingly unexpected discovery.

We were later informed that his condition had improved enough for him to be released to go home. He was taken to relatives until he adjusted to his new lifestyle and after several days I stopped by for a visit. As I was invited in, the Starrer was sitting on the side of the bed where he was laying. She was sitting beside him with gifts thrown across the bed and I had a front row seat to it all, but I wasn't taking this anymore! He welcomed me into the room, smiling and behaving as though he didn't have a care in the world. I asked him, "What is going on?" and he said, "She came by to check on me and to bring me something?" I asked, "Why?" He began to tell me how I knew the situation and therefore should not have a problem with it. He was arrogant enough to believe that he could have the both of us and said so with complete confidence! I couldn't believe what he was suggesting, nor would it be something I would accept any longer! I had allowed the madness to go on for far too long but now I had to consider what was best for my child. It was one thing when it was me, although I should not have accepted it then. I then told him, "I will not be a part of this and I won't allow my child to either!" He had no expression one way or the other in regards to my comment and I simply walked out and didn't look back! Where had this strength come from and why had it taken so long for me to say enough?

CHAPTER 5

Death and more Death

Again, another destructive chapter of my life had finally been closed with a man who had no intentions of living for anyone other than himself. I had finally decided that we were definitely better off without him in our lives. I had made a tough decision for someone other than myself and my mind was made up that my child would not live through the same madness and disconnect I had! I was moving on with my life and my child and I were taking a different route this time! Through this entire time that I was making trips to see the Donor Dad, Mr. Good Guy was watching my child endlessly without complaints. He treated him as though he was his biological child, loved him through his actions and not just words. He had shown an indescribable attachment to my child and now he was equally attached to me. He was no longer seeing the other woman that I believed he would never get over and it appeared he too had decided to choose a different route. He started coming around more often, spending lots of time with us, and we really enjoyed one another's company. I had a great admiration for him because he had been so good to me and my child, despite being placed on the back burner during my Donor Dad involvement.

Then as our courtship progressed, I found out I was pregnant again, but couldn't really say how I felt one way or the other, however I knew Mr. Good Guy would be a great Dad! He had already demonstrated his ability through my child who he had practically raised just as my Daddy did with my siblings. Mr. Good Guy loved our son and as the pregnancy progressed, I continued to deal with his confusion and my own. Many times I would catch the bus to the doctor to step off of it and see him and the other woman in his car patiently waiting for the bus to move on down the road. He was picking up the other woman as I caught the bus to go to the doctor carrying his child. I couldn't understand what had happened to this responsible, loving and giving man, yet again I knew what blind love would drive a person to do or not do! On November 10, 1983, I was taken to the hospital at thirty six weeks of my pregnancy because I had an unusual feeling. I couldn't explain the feeling; I just knew that something wasn't right. As Mr. Good Guy, Mama, the Young One and I arrived at the hospital, the Doctor began examining me. Although, he put forth every effort to hide his facial expressions, I immediately noticed how solace he had become after the exam was complete. He searched and searched for a heartbeat and then asked me, "When was the last time you felt the baby move?" I said with great hesitation and panic, "I don't remember!" He proceeded to have the nurses come in and moved me to another ward alone, however before doing so he compassionately explained, "I cannot find your baby's heartbeat." I was thinking, "What does that mean exactly?" It just couldn't mean what I thought and he couldn't be telling me what I was feeling!

As they rolled my hospital bed to the empty ward they began to explain to me that they were going to induce my labor so that I could deliver my dead child! I felt like a zombie and was in complete and utter disbelief and an aching pain filled my entire body and I too was dead from the inside out! As the dreadful process of being stuck with needles for the IV and the medications began to run their course, I was emotionless! The ward was cold, dark and quiet with no one walking or talking around me and I didn't know how to feel or what to do after discovering I had been left alone to deliver my beautiful child! The pain as a result of the medications started to take affect and my body was doing what it was being forced to do, and I began to go to that place that I would go as a wounded child! The pain within me was being brought on by more than medication for it was the deepest, heart wrenching, and painful wound within my heart of knowing I would not hear my baby cry, feel the warmth of her touch, or look into her eyes, and I would not be taking her home with me. As the process continued I began to get angry, but the contractions were getting closer and closer and the intensity forced me to begin to push, push, and push as my heart would break into more and more pieces with each push!

As I continued to push in the lonely, dark, and cold room, I waited to see when someone was going to come in to offer me any words of comfort, but no one came. Why was no one there with me during this dreadful, heart breaking and indescribable moment? Finally, the dreadful moment had arrived and the lifeless tiny body lay between my legs, but I never rose up to take a look or even a glance, because I just couldn't stand the idea of seeing my child lying there motionless. I just couldn't! As I laid there with my child between my legs lifeless, and without anyone present for only God knows how long. The Doctor finally entered from behind the curtain to witness that I had delivered my stillborn baby and he became livid and started shouting, "Why would any of you leave her by herself knowing that she was delivering a stillborn child?!" Then he proceeded to remove my baby from between my legs and turned to exit the door, but sadly before exiting he said, "It's a girl." As he took her away I still could not look or receive his words because I didn't want to believe this was really happening! How could it be and what had I done wrong this time? He returned shortly thereafter and proceeded to explain that I would have to push the afterbirth out too, but it felt more like the after-death to me! She was not alive and therefore the usage of his normal delivery verbiage shook me to my core!

As they moved me back into a more populated area of the hospital, the Doctor pulled the curtains back a second time and stepped in with my beautifully wrapped daughter in his arms and placed her in my arms. As I looked into her beautiful, dark skinned, angelic face the tears began to fall uncontrollably. My Mama, the Young One, and Mr. Good Guy entered the area with little to nothing to say, although there was nothing that they could have said that would have soothed my pain. After the staff allowed us time to spend with her, the Doctor then informed me due to her five pound two ounce weight we were responsible for her burial arrangements. The loss was just simply not enough and now they have told me that I had to make funeral arrangements! This child that I had loved inside of me for thirty six weeks, this child who shared my breath, this child who was no more would have to be eulogized and hadn't even lived! I was asked to provide them with the funeral home that I would like for them to contact to come and pick up her remains and I was discharged the very next day. Before leaving as I was looking outside the window into the sky, the hospital's Chaplin attempted to offer me comfort through various scriptures in the Bible. I didn't even respond or acknowledge her presence until she asked me an unusual question. "Are you angry with God," she asked and I didn't know how I felt but I knew that question was not making me feel better! I was grieving a tremendous loss no one should have to endure and she continued asking me ridiculous questions! She kept telling me, "God loves you and He loves your daughter too." She continued to say, "Trust Him and believe that He knows what is best for you and He'll never leave or forsake you." I looked back at her and burst into tears and she walked over and placed her arms out to comfort me.

A few days later as we were getting prepared to make final arrangements at the funeral home for the burial of my Angel, I was in enormous pain both physically and mentally! As we entered the funeral home, the Funeral Director was a compassionate and loving woman whose empathy showed through the smile that she greeted us with. She took charge as though she could read my every thought and assured me that I would be satisfied with her service. She gave me confidence and security knowing that she would take care of my precious daughter as though she were her own. I then left to go and find something beautiful for my daughter to be buried in. Mrs. Good Intentions offered to do it for me but showed up with two simple and plain blouses considering her normal extravagant taste. The wound burned even deeper when Mama said to me, "I wouldn't bury my dog in that!" I was livid with them both for their inconsiderate actions and words! How could she dress us up so lavish for Easter year after year yet brought something simple for my precious daughter? The thought hurt me and poured salt on an already open wound! Why did she want to bury my child as though she were unimportant?

I began to search despite being told that I needed to stay home. I looked for the best dress for my little Angel that I could find and was able to find what I wanted right down to the ruffle socks and shoes for her little tiny feet. Then, I dropped them back off at the funeral home and was again greeted by the Director who said, "Oh, how beautiful!" Her reaction pleased me deeply for she had given me that lift I so desperately needed through all this pain! On November 15, 1984 we prepared for her home going service and I found myself back in zombie mode thinking, "Is this really happening?" I was eighteen years old and trying to be strong, but the pain was so deep and intense that I didn't know what to do next. The home going service was short and sweet although I didn't remember much about it other than her pink casket with satin and lace with her tiny body lying there as though she were asleep. As the service drew to an end it was off to her final resting place on earth and then we went back to Mama's with a few close friends and very little family present. As the day progressed my friends were trying to do everything to take my mind off of my sweet baby and one even asked, "May I give you a makeover?" I agreed but no makeup in the world was going to cover up this pain! This pain was there and didn't seem as though it would ever leave me. Would I stay in this dreadful place forever and if so would I come out of it the same?

CHAPTER 6

Mixed Emotions

I t was eight days after the day of my Angel's burial and Mr. Good Guy had decided he wanted to marry me and I thought I wanted the same thing. More so, I wanted to do anything to make the dreadful, awful, and piercing pain go away! We decided to go to the Pastor of close relatives and because of their commitment to the church he married us at their request. He didn't know us, counsel us, or instruct us in regards to the sincerity of the vows we were preparing to take, but I've often wondered would it have made a difference? The root of our problems in the marriage was created by us. Mr. Good Guy did some things that caused us to drift apart, but the decisions I made were those of my own desire because I was only thinking of me and no one but me! Sound familiar? I just wanted and needed the pain to disappear, but even greater than that I wanted my baby to be with me! I wanted to understand something that was not for me to understand! I was young and as we left the church to head to Mama's where I was living, we were reminded of how little thought was put into this huge decision for he too lived with his Mother. Mama had prepared a mini reception at our house of which was quite a pleasant surprise because she was ready to celebrate our union. It wasn't expected or anticipated but much appreciated and all present had a good time.

As time passed and we quickly approached the end of the year and almost two months into the New Year, it was placed heavily on my heart the need to go and see my Daddy. I would always have those feelings with Daddy and I would have a tantrum until someone took me to see him; this weekend was no different. Daddy was in good spirit, cracking jokes, and drinking his brew of choice, yet was asking some unusual questions of me. One of the questions that he asked that really stuck out was when he said, "Black gal, are you happy?" Without thought, I quickly answered, "Yes!" I had done something that I had never done before to Daddy, but I didn't want him to be concerned about the woes in my marriage. I felt so guilty that I had not told him the truth, but I had already kept so many secrets from him to protect him. I wanted to protect him and give him the security he had always provided for me, but the guilt remained. I was always honest with Daddy, respected him, and didn't want to do anything to tarnish his admiration for me. Why didn't I tell him I wasn't happy in the marriage?

After visiting all day and having a great time, as always, we headed back home from the country. I called Daddy to inform him that I would see him the next weekend and he was excited and looked forward to it as much as me. To my dismay and heartbreak, the following morning I received a call from Mr. Mellow Fellow who asked me, "Are you home alone?" I hesitantly told him, "No, Mr. Good Guy is outside," but before he could say another word an overwhelming, stabbing pain came over me, and I braced myself for what he was about to tell me. He proceeded to say, "I'm so sorry, but they found your Daddy dead this morning." I dropped the phone and began running towards the door. Mr. Good Guy came running and asked me, "What's wrong?" Upon telling him, he too was in the same state of shock as me; absolute devastation! We had just left him the evening before and talked with him on the phone upon our arrival home, so how could he be dead? My world was crumbling into pieces all around me and now once again my mind had begun to play tricks on me. My daughter and my Daddy only months apart, how could this be? I then believed this was a ploy that Mama had created to keep me from seeing my Daddy. She just couldn't accept the relationship that we shared and reminded me often of how much I was like him! It took four days and the arrival of the Scary Little Boy from his military duties to force me back into the land of reality! I just couldn't believe or accept that Daddy was gone, but when the Scary Little Boy stepped out of the corridor from his flight home, reality hit me like a ton of bricks! I knew the military would not send him home on a ruse. What in the world do I do now that my rock is gone? Who would be there to love me without terms and conditions? Who? Daddy was gone and Mr. Good Guy was trying to comfort me the best he knew how, but I didn't want his comfort; I wanted my Daddy! The path of self-destruction had raised its ugly head once again and I just didn't care!

As we prepared for Daddy's funeral the following weekend, I stepped into the limousine as we traveled to the church and stepped out to enter into the church. I couldn't even walk down the aisle to his casket for this was another heartbreaking misery that had entered my life. The service was a blur for I was there in body but my mind was gone to that far away place. After the service ended we headed to the cemetery, and as the final words were given by the funeral Director they were packing me off; I just couldn't take another step without him. My Daddy and my Angel both had left me and I was all alone again. I didn't want them to leave me but what was I to do because they were gone? Daddy, why had you left me, who would I trust, who would love me unconditionally, and who would be honest with me rather I liked it or not? The ones I loved were gone and they weren't coming back! Mr. Good Guy was trying to help me in every way that he could, but he just could not reach that place of anguish. My sweet son would occasionally succeed in putting a smile on my face, but most times I was so engulfed in sorrow he could only wipe the tears from my eyes. I was on the edge of the cliff and I just wanted to jump, but he continued to shower his innocent love on me.

Months passed and I was just running wild and acting as though I had lost my mind which was exactly how I felt. Time continued to pass and once again no menstrual cycle and I was pregnant! It was my third child and I was only twenty years old and the fear of this pregnancy had already started to set in. I really wanted this child for Mr. Good Guy and me, although he had others, they weren't with me. He had fathered one child before we met and that child's Mother was saying, "My new baby is his too!" He initially denied it but it came to light as the child grew older in age. He had an older child who I loved as my own and who loved me, but the younger child did not take to me because of outside negative opinions regarding me. I wanted to be their Mother because I knew they needed me and I wanted the best for them despite some minor issues between me and their biological

Mother. As they grew so much went on in their lives that created more tension in our marriage, yet I still loved them and knew I always would! I had a terrific gynecologist who knew and understood my fears from the stillbirth and was extremely accommodating; going above and beyond his call of duty. The pregnancy was going good and I was so focused on having a healthy baby, nothing else seemed to matter including Mr. Good Guy. I did everything the doctor said and followed his medical direction to the letter. This was the most disciplined I had been in many years considering how out of control my life had been to this point.

In June 1985, I arrived at the hospital and Mrs. Good Intentions was already there and entered into the examination room with me. As the Doctor prepared for the delivery there was a brief moment of leeriness when he told me, "Your sack has been leaking and we need to get the baby out of there!" Despite his calm demeanor, I could see his concern, and I was eager for them to get busy. He reentered, broke my water sack, and shortly thereafter my lovely child made her entrance into the world. Another medication free delivery, lovely, bright-eyed, and my beautiful child looked up at me, however due to the sack leaking, the Doctor informed me that she had to be taken to the neonatal intensive care unit to be monitored. The Doctor allowed me to be taken by wheelchair to see her to reassure me that she was in good condition. I was excited, nervous, and concerned, but thankful as I watched the nurses smiling and admiring her feistiness. After being examined from head to toe the Doctor cleared us to go home in two days and we brought her home. I was thankful beyond words, but still had mixed emotions. I didn't consider her a replacement of my Heavenly Angel, yet thanked God for the blessing of a healthy and happy child. Then it was back to trying to be the perfect wife and mother, sometimes even taking on the motherly role with Mr. Good Guy, but after a while, it was no longer a role I was willing to play with him and decided I would leave again. I had left once before and returned thinking my leaving would have made a difference, but it didn't!

I still had many of the same behaviors, and no adjustments had been made by either of us. Eventually, we drifted in different paths despite the fact that we loved one another. He was always working to provide for his family, but spending no time with us and therefore left me playing dual roles. He was doing so much more than my eyes could or wanted to see because of the pain that dwelled within. I later returned once again, but that time, I had convinced myself it was for the sake of our children. We continued from where we left off and although much of what he felt was genuine love for me, I felt more obligation than love for him. He didn't deserve much of what I had taken him through in this union and I was unfaithful throughout. With all that he did and sacrificed for us, it just never was enough for me because I didn't know what I needed or wanted and questioned if I ever had. I couldn't share with him much of the pain that he was trying his best to fill or eliminate. I had so many regrets but what was done had been done and the most I could offer were my apologies and his pleasure; sex. As we continued to have our intimate relations I became pregnant with our fourth child but I did not want another child. I was so confused and miserable that I didn't want to bring another child into this misery, but an abortion was out of the question!

Mr. Good Guy had become even more driven by his work and every other aspect of the responsibilities was completely on me. I waited five months before I was finally persuaded by a friend that I needed to go to the doctor. I took her advice and went to receive confirmation of what I already knew. I was working so hard at making our marriage work, yet the idea of another baby to care for plunged me into a temporary state of depression. In February 1987, our youngest child was born without complications and we were released to go home the next day. However, instead of home, we were invited to stay at the home of Mr. Good Guy's mother during my recovery, and although her offer was greatly appreciated, it was short lived because of his work. I was back to my dual roles and every aspect of our family had fallen right back on my shoulders. We had many discussions regarding him becoming more involved, but the more I talked the less he did. I decided to leave for the final time and the time had come that I would not be coming back. The children were young but old enough that they understood the toll it was taking on our family. My track record had proved I was not good in this relationship or any other for that matter. Fortunately, we were blessed to part ways and continued to show our children we still shared a close friendship after the marriage.

Even after we were gone and he realized we weren't going to return, he never once told me, "I don't have any money or I'll have to pay you later." As well, we never had to go through the Attorney General's office to force him to provide for our children. We sat down and made a mutual agreement in regards to their support and it was binding, because it was our word! I was not out to get him for he truly was a good guy. He had been with us; just differently. He came faithfully to pick them up and spent lots of time with them, so it was as though he was still there as far as the children were concerned. Even when I lost the apartment the children and I were living in due to my recklessness, I never told him a word in regards to it. I sent two of my children to stay with my Mama, and the other to stay with a close relative that I trusted as I lived in my car. Yes, I was homeless, but it was by choice because I didn't want to hear another negative thing regarding my irresponsibility from anyone. In a matter of one week, I hustled harder than I ever had in my life to get my business straight so I could be back with my children! Not to mention the shame I would have had if I told Mr. Good Guy that I chose to live in my car compared to at least calling on him for additional assistance. I never told him or anyone my living conditions; instead I allowed them to think whatever they wanted of me. It wasn't as though they thought good of me most of the time anyway, but that was no excuse to allow pride, shame, and stubbornness to separate me from my children for any length of time and it never happened again!

CHAPTER 7

Hard to Say Goodbye

I had left for the final time and I was trying to find my own, despite being told by family and friends that I was a fool for leaving Mr. Good Guy. They only saw what I allowed them to see; therefore I was not staying for them and had not left for them! We moved into several different apartment complexes through the years and I moved from job to job through staffing agencies or friend referrals. I continued working in joints, hustling on the pool table, and manipulating men because I didn't want to let go of what I felt I couldn't. I continued dealing with some of the same issues with Mama as an adult that I had dealt with as a child, but I just wanted to try to restore our relationship. Many times it was very difficult for me and I was certain she felt the same way. Just as we would make progress, something would happen that would knock us backwards all over again. I was so angry from the past, that it didn't take much for me to just give up on my efforts. Why were these feelings still within me and why didn't I realize that I had made little to no progress? Why hadn't I reached out for help and if I had, would it have made a difference? This had been a battle within for practically my entire life and I was fearful of the rejection or judgment of my confessions to anyone!

Mama and I had made tremendous progress in our relationship and we were communicating several times a day. As she prepared for a trip to a wedding in the Hill Country, I called from work to make certain she had gone and arrived home safely from her hair appointment. She was excited about attending the wedding the upcoming weekend and being able to see many of her old friends. As the phone rang, one of my children answered her phone. I asked, "What are you doing at your Grandma's house?" She replied, "Daddy came to pick her up to take her to the hospital." I said, "Take her to the hospital for what? I demanded, "Let me talk to Mama!" Upon her arrival to the phone, I asked her, "Baby, what's wrong?" She replied, "My back is killing me!" I was puzzled for we had just spoke hours earlier and she was fine, so I immediately informed my supervisor and left for the hospital. As I arrived, they had just taken her in from Mr. Good Guy's car and as I walked into the triage, she was sitting up in the bed smiling as though she felt better, but instead was admitted into the hospital. It was fourteen days later and she appeared to be getting progressively worse. I became totally fed up with the little effort on the behalf of the medical professionals to find out what was making her so sick I asked her, "What do you want me to do?" She said, "I want to go home!" I said, "Mama, you're really sick and we need to find out what is wrong with you!"

She was adamant about going home, so we agreed that if I took her out of there, she would allow me to take her to another doctor in a couple of days. It was a stormy Friday evening and it was her and I and they didn't want to release her. My anger and protective mode kicked in full throttle! I wasn't going to be stopped by anything or anyone from honoring her request, especially considering they hadn't done anything to help her at that point! They even had the nerve to call a hospital security officer up to Mama's ward to have me removed from the hospital! As I stood there prepared to rumble, I told him, "It will take more than you to keep me from taking her out of here, this is the only Mother I have!" He said, "Ma'am, I understand." Then he left the room and I proceeded to continuing what we agreed she wanted; to go home. As it continued to storm outside, I stepped out of her room to find a wheel chair and returned to then lift her into the chair and out to my car we went. The nurse began running behind me to get me to sign her discharge papers.

Two days passed since I had brought her home and she was still quite ill, but I couldn't get a doctor to see her until the next day. Since the most they had told us what that she had a large mass throughout her body, I contacted an Oncologist to see her to get some definite answers and explanations as to how she went from preparing for a trip to hardly able to stand on her own! I took her to the Oncologist and as we sat in the waiting room, I looked around at all the people with no hair, fail looking, and I began to think, "This will not be my Mama!" She would not go through this, however upon seeing the doctor, he immediately admitted her into another hospital. As I drove her over in my car, they were waiting on our arrival and wheeled her off for immediate supervised care. She remained at that hospital and they were still dumb-founded as to what was going on with her. With all the technology that they had why couldn't they tell us something? The day had come and she was moved to yet another hospital and on the fourth day she was diagnosed with cancer of an unknown origin, and her prognosis was nine months to a year. She had cancer and things went from bad to worse when they told her and we were not in the room with her! This was one of her greatest fears and now they were telling her that she had this disease in her body. I yelled, "You just killed her by putting it in her mind!"

She was fighting so hard, but before long she didn't even want me to wheel her downstairs to smoke a cigarette. She had started hallucinating on the morphine drip and told me all sorts of things that I had heard others talk about when someone felt they were dying. She was saying so much but I was trying to keep her focused on getting better. It wasn't three months after her initial first trip to the hospital that she was dead! I had just been there two days prior and she was still trying to tell me, but I couldn't stand to hear it. She was trying to prepare me for her final departure, but I missed it because I didn't want it to be! I was informed by Mrs. Good Intentions after I received a call from her trying to prevent me from coming to the hospital, but I kept questioning her until she was forced to tell me. I was trying to get her off the phone to get to the hospital and she was trying to keep me from being caught off guard, yet again I wasn't listening. I began to think back to what Mama was trying to prepare me for with the many words she said, but why had she chosen me to tell so much? As the words from Mrs. Good Intentions and Mama sank into my head, I dropped to my knees for the thought had never crossed my mind that she would actually die! It wasn't as though she was invincible, but I just didn't think her illness was so bad or I didn't want to think it! No child wants to bury their parents no matter what they may have gone through with them, yet this heart—aching moment had entered into my already torn down world.

Mama had one specific request that she spoke continually regarding her children; she wanted us to be close and not divided. As I had my man of the moment rush me to the hospital, I once again walked into regret. There was no one from the family there when I arrived so I went to the nurse's station and asked, "Where is my Mother?" The nurse looked at me and stood to offer her condolences and directed me to the room where she laid dead! As I entered, the curtain was drawn and I moved it from my view to see her there with a look that I would never forget; complete exhaustion! They had combed her hair back into a pony tail and the sheet was pulled to her collar bone and tucked neatly on both sides of her and she was ice cold to the touch. I talked to her saying, "Mama, you don't have to suffer anymore. All the heartaches of this world are over; now you can finally rest." As these words came from my mouth, I began to reflect on the many previous conversations we had. She had told me goodbye and had passed the family's burden of division in my lap. She wanted me to know that she loved me and trusted that I would put forth every effort of keeping the family together just as she desired. After the extremely difficult task of walking out of the room and going to the waiting area to wait on the Funeral home's staff to arrive to pick up her remains. I called my supervisor to tell her that she was gone for she had been so supportive the entire time. Once again another part of me had died all over again and I didn't know what would come next. As I sat there and watched the elevator door open, out walked the Tiny One to extend his comfort to me despite dealing with his own dreadful pain.

The Tiny One was fragile, confused, kind hearted and had always been around Mama from the time he was a premature baby. He had a special bond with her and shared that same closeness with me. He was always concerned for our well-being and lived with us more often than not. He was another one of my children and I raised him as such. He battled with confusion for many years and was trying to find his way through the toils and turns of his troublesome life. After leaving the hospital, I called my Pastor and then immediately requested to be taken to my Godmother's home. As I entered the door, my Godfather sat at the dining room table next to his oxygen pump and I informed him that Mama was gone. He was so humble, loving, and supportive as he had always been and then my Godmother arrived home from church service to comfort me with her words and the Word of God. I had been a part of this family for many years and always felt the love that beamed from their sincerity. My God sister and I shared a very close bond of the few people I had known in my entire life and was the most dependable, supportive, and loving sister I had been blessed with. I was dealing with many different emotions, concerns, and guilt, but I knew she had tried to let me know that she had freed me from the acts of my foolishness from the past.

The next day, Mrs. Good Intentions, Mrs. Sanctified and I arrived and met the Funeral Director to make her final arrangements. Mrs. Sanctified was a miserable, negative, and dual personality woman who despite our closeness in earlier years, I found it easier to keep my distance. Surprisingly, I was pleased because we were in agreement just as Mama wanted and there was no one trying to do more than the other. We just wanted to bury her with the dignity that she deserved. It was a difficult time for me because I knew things in my life were in for a major change! Mama was the glue that held the family together despite her woes, and these shoes would not be easily filled. As we all prepared a few days later for her viewing and funeral, all went as well as could be expected. Mama's home going was spirit-filled just as she wanted and then to the cemetery we traveled for her burial. Most of the family came to the repast, but some went their separate ways; the division had already started just as she knew it would. She told me so much because she knew who would do and who wouldn't.

The next day some of us gathered at Mama's to decide on what to do with all her belongings for we had plenty of our own. Mrs. Sanctified received a telephone call from a person who was not in attendance at Mama's service yet wanted to come by to create havoc. Mrs. Sanctified welcomed her and upon her arrival, the Tiny One was trying to prevent anything from escalating from this surprise visit, but so much for those efforts. As I walked briefly into Mama's home after grabbing the Tiny One's child from the Drama Mama and back outside, I had stepped into the Twilight Zone! Mrs. Sanctified was in the yard pulling the Other Mama's hair and clowning to no end and I was in utter disbelief, shocked, and couldn't believe what I was witnessing! Why was this madness happening the day after

Mama's burial and what was gained from this ridiculous behavior? Why had she initiated this confrontation that was preventable and even become a part of it? As I cried and screamed for my children to get in the truck I knew our relationship had changed in the blink of an eye! I just couldn't and didn't understand why this had happened! What had I lost now from witnessing this madness and how could they dishonor Mama's memory in such a way? After I left, I returned the next day to sort through Mama's belongings, but my mind was still focused on the prior day's fiasco.

Everyone was gone and I was left to sort through the memories of the Mama that I desired to know more about. I asked myself, "What now?" She had left everything but only a few reminders as to what to do next. She was supposed to live beyond her mere sixty seven years or so my finite mind believed. "Mama, what do I do now?" The mayhem had already begun and I was not in a good place because of it, yet I had to try to honor her request of me. As the days turned to weeks, and the weeks to months, and the months to years, I was going to the cemetery every Sunday after church service as though she was there. It was my only place of peace as I would lay on Mama's grave and flood the dirt with my tears. The bond that she desired to remain intact had fallen to pieces rapidly! Did she know it would get this way so fast and why was there so little willingness to honor her as we continued to remain divided?

CHAPTER 8

The More Things Change,
The More They Stay The Same

As we continued going on with our lives separately, spending little to no time with one another; other than the times Scary Little Boy or I would extend an invitation to an occasion or holiday gathering at our homes. Sometimes, everyone would actually show up. All the years that had passed, yet this was our unfortunate reality and everyone seemed to be comfortable right where they were. Although, Mama was gone and we were all grown men and women, it showed drastically how in depth the effects the untold secrets had affected each of our lives. I had not believed for one second that this was only my story, however apparently I had been the one chosen to speak my voice. Mama had shared so much with me as her life was coming to an end and she was extremely concerned at the thought of what would happen with us; her children and grandchildren. She felt that I would be the one that would have to put forth the effort of keeping us close and had passed the baton to me, but I didn't want it! Our conversations would replay over and over in my head and I could feel the pain in my heart, yet I thought if I could live up to her expectation, I would finally do something to please her; even in death.

We were her legacy and she understood the loneliness of being without siblings to share that special bond or connection with because she was an only child. She desperately wanted us to connect, however the division had been created through the years and the inability of accepting one another for who we were. I realized how deep our separation had become when I began doing my personal analysis. In addition to looking at myself, I began to see what pain and heartache was spread throughout our family by actions and not just words. Much of our care through the years was placed in the lap of Mrs. Good Intentions despite her not wanting or deserving it. She would come across abrasive, angry, stand offish, dominate, defensive, and yet still compassionate. She didn't deserve the responsibility regardless to the fact that we were related, but she expected much in return for her sometimes undesired sacrifices.

I was always puzzled by her because she would give you the shirt off her back, yet there were visible signs of her feelings of frustration and pain that could be felt from miles away. Those feelings had been felt by me for many, many years, regardless to the numerous attempts of trying to get close to her. She would try so hard to keep her emotions hidden and I knew that same feeling because I had done so for so long! She doesn't call often unless she is in need of a favor, or she wants to inform me of something that may be of benefit to her. She instead prefers the modern day method of texting and then she can be short regarding whatever it is she wants to relay. It really bothered me the fact that she found it easier to communicate through text, but then I didn't like the voice of disgust I would hear through the phone line either. Was that an excuse and if so, why had it continued to be like that? She never minded working very hard behind the scenes, but then complained about not receiving recognition. I knew deep within she really wanted to do everything that she did, yet I questioned the motives for her doing them. I had no other choice because that was all she had shown me. She was prideful and I believed that stemmed from early childhood years, but she refused to give into her true inner being. She preferred to keep her distance and I felt she did most things out of obligation rather than love. This was a part of the acceptance she needed from those around her and I just wanted to be around her. I had told her on many occasions, "I love you," yet she couldn't give into expressing those words to me. She was a loving and caring woman, but I recognized the pain that only allowed her true being to escape in rare instances.

It pained me for I had no doubts that we could help one another, but she chose to shut down and not talk about much of anything with me from her past to assist me with questions from mine. It was like that with all of us and God only knew what secrets lye within that continued to keep us quiet. The silence had kept us imprisoned and divided for years and it was affecting the next generations coming behind us. As often as I had reached out, I had been rejected twice as much. Although, there were memories of happy times that I tightly held on to, yet they were few and far between. When I had been ill, which was often, her concern for me appeared genuine, but confusion was still there because she didn't show her emotions, instead she felt her presence was enough and I accepted what I could get. She had taken me on trips where we had so much fun that I didn't want it to end, because I knew once we returned home the fairy tale was over. They were memories I would never forget because that was the woman I knew lived deep inside her pain. She wanted to be set free and could I have helped her or would she have been swallowed in the depth of the sorrow and pain that had plagued her and our family for so long?

Mrs. Long Distance had been far from home since I was around four or five years old. She was passive, troubled, plagued with illness, and the mirror image of Mama. She married and moved out of state but was kept informed of each family moment through Mama until her death. She struggled with many battles, but would sacrifice to meet the needs of someone else over her own. She over compensated because of the void in her heart due to the past in many areas of her life. I falsely believed it was easier for her because of the distance to tolerate the division, but it wasn't long before I discovered that could not be further from the truth. She yearned for the absence of family despite the distance and I began to communicate with her more frequently. I didn't want her to feel as I had and tried to encourage her, but I could not explain behavior to her that I didn't understand myself. I tried to assist her in understanding that we couldn't allow other's actions to affect ours. She always said, "I love you", but I also knew that could change like the weather. We both had felt mixed emotions that were often times fueled by others when they were upset with someone else in the family. Everyone wanted things their way, under their conditions, or you were out of there! Wouldn't it be lovely if everyone cared and loved without limitations, terms, and conditions? She has tried with every fiber of her being to be set free, but the pain and heartache seems to consume her.

Mrs. Sanctified and I were the closest in my teens, twenties and early thirties. She had a beautiful dark complexion, smart, witty, and a need to be needed. We were there for one another even when times were tough, but some time shortly after Mama's death, things began to go sour. She had been talking God's Word to me for years, despite knowing that she too was putting on the same façade I had. She was not in the best relationships from my eyes, but it was her life, her entitlement and I tried to support her. Many times because of our bond, I would get drawn in to protect her without taking any consideration for my own well-being. Her relationships were abusive; mentally and physically, and she lacked the security in herself that I always saw. Whenever I would go out to her rescue, it never bothered me one way or the other because I wanted to protect her. She could smile and light up a room when she entered, but would become extremely upset when any conversing pertaining to her past entered the conversation. She had even gone so far as to say, "That's why I don't come around!"

We would many times joke to find some kind of humor to hide the pain, but since no one really knew anyone else's, how could we have known how deep the jokes were cutting her? We would have a free for all that would include everyone, but she never considered any part of these moments funny or entertaining. Before long her visits had become fewer and fewer and then they totally stopped, and it became pleading with her to be in our company. She had an overwhelming negative cloud that hung over her head and although it had been addressed, it changed none the less. The phone calls stopped too, because she felt that if she were important enough, I would call her. Before I knew it, she was out of my life and the rare occasions that I was in her presence, she gave me looks that I really believed she didn't think I saw, and feelings she didn't believe I felt. It was like daggers in my heart considering how often she had said, "I love you!" Real love doesn't feel like this, shouldn't feel like this, and doesn't look like this! I had often wondered where I had gone wrong, but what untold secrets and pains must her weary soul be hiding and doesn't want anyone to know?

Scary Little Boy and I spent most of our lives together, although he had many memories that were far from those of mine. He was very intelligent, a geek, strongly opinioned, and a kid at heart. I often told him, "You have a memory like an elephant!" I couldn't even imagine what memories must be locked in the center of his soul. We attended the same schools because he was a year and a half older than me and I dared anyone to touch him! I was the fighter and he was the book worm, although he had his daredevil moments that left Mama concerned for him many years. He was a womanizer and I would become so angry with him to a point that we would physically fight, however he could cut with words better than any fist fight I ever had. We became distant for a few years due to my opinions and involvement in his relationships that I didn't belong in. Who was I to talk considering the mess I had made with my own life? He wasn't bothered in the least by our teasing him of his lengthy lineage because he was a proud father of ten children, despite his mistakes. It pained me to see how some of our family felt towards him because of those very errors that we had all made. It was amazing to me how quickly we could find fault in everyone else before looking at ourselves. He went to the military straight out of high school and returned home a proud man; as well he should. There was still distance between us but when he would reach out; I would reach back.

He was never short of words and when I or any of us are on his good side, he made us feel like the best in the world, but that other side is not a pleasant visitor; I have taken many blows below the belt. As the years had come and gone, I had seen his sincere effort to change from many of those old behaviors to some positive ones, yet he still dealt with the rejection from those he desired to love him most. I had watched him make choices out of anger that contributed greatly to the additional separation within the family. He tried so hard, but the devil knew his weaknesses and preyed on them with a vengeance. He wanted the same we all wanted; to be loved! He was accustomed to lashing out when he was hurt by anyone because of his inner battle. He continued to battle, but is strong and stubborn enough to not give up! He spoke strength in regards to his troubled relationships with our family and friends, but I knew it pained his heart deeply. I had seen the change in him when he humbled himself with tears pouring down before an audience of people to apologize to my husband because he misjudged him. The tears fell from his and my eyes uncontrollably because he stepped out and did something that he didn't have to do. He made a conscience choice to right a wrong, and I had not forgotten what it meant that he was willing to put himself aside for someone else. He could be selfish and focus only on himself, but he had demonstrated his willingness to step into his new space.

The Young One grew up outside of the household with other family members, but eventually came back and lived with us when I was thirteen years old. He was small, cute, spoiled, sweet, and humorous. Mama had a special place in her heart towards him and I often referred to him as family favorite in our latter years. He was the one that it appeared missed out on the madness too, but I was wrong yet again. After high school, he also enlisted in the military and returned home to some of the same things he had left. He lived a little bit of everywhere; including Hawaii for several years and was a funny man at heart. He moved back to the Lone Star state and occasionally invited us to visit for special occasions. He often traveled home for visits, but I usually found out once he had already come and gone. He too was not excluded from his share of mistakes, but continued to strive to be who he had such admiration for; Mr. Mellow Fellow. He was our Father figure and represented the sacrifices a man made for his family through the good and bad times. He was God fearing, calm-spirited, humble, and strong. I wasn't always there to see some things, but I knew he knew the Lord personally. I could see his light shining when I couldn't understand how it could. Mr. Mellow Fellow had been the same regardless of anyone else's opinion and if he was swayed; he hid it well.

He had told us stories of his earlier years that were fascinating because we thought he could do no wrong. He wanted us to see through him that God could change anyone's life that was willing to give their life to Him. I understood why the Young One had so much respect towards him, because he showed respect toward us. Often times, the Young One could portray himself in a way that he had everything together, but I could see through him like a window pane. When plans were made that pertained to him and "his" family as he would say, he would expect everyone to drop everything to accommodate his request. When anyone had other plans opposite that of his, he would consider it to be an unwillingness to sacrifice for him and took it personally when deep within he knew that wasn't true, yet it was the truth that he preferred to believe. For so many years I believed we all sacrificed something for the sake of family, but at some point when had the sacrifice for family not been enough? He called with his bubbly personality and usually always lifted my spirit with his energy, but I sometimes questioned the sincerity of the calls. I knew and understood that he was often encouraging me through his own pain and appreciated his efforts. He too had questions but not even he was willing to seek answers. I had no doubts our family was full of secrets and I knew this was not just my story; it was ours!

I realized whole-heartedly that it was easier said than done to remove something that had been a part of me for so long, but the painful reality of life kept moving on. My destructive behavior continued because I believed it was the only release that I could come up with to cope with the grief and anything else. There was so much left unsaid, and there was so much that needed to be told, but was too late? My world had fallen apart around me yet no one could recognize the signs; not even me! I was in another relationship that I believed to be going pretty well until I wanted to do as I had always been able to. I did not need or want a Father, but did need a partner and understanding companion because I still was undecided if I wanted someone there all the time. Along came Mr. Athlete who accommodated that need and the relationship started when a friend introduced us. He was muscular, tall, dark and handsome, yet lacked the confidence that was appealing to me in a man. Although, it started just as I desired, he began showing signs of jealousy that I attempted ignoring, but before long he was really serious and demonstrated some undesirable behaviors. I was still doing my thing with Mr. Good Guy as I had for over fifteen years because I still loved him, I could, and because I wanted to. Mr. Athlete's assumed confidence had passed and his insecurities had come to a head and he was no longer what I wanted in a relationship; temporary or otherwise! I wanted a strong, secure, and understanding yet gentle man like Daddy! As I made the decision and told him the relationship was over, he appeared to be satisfied with that resolve as long as we could remain friends.

How foolish of me to believe it would be that simple when I had seen his behavior in regards to me with other men! He was telling me and anyone in my inner circle that would listen how much he loved me and to please talk to me. He began showing up on my job unannounced, damaging my vehicle, paying for the repairs, and he even followed me two hours out of the city! I hadn't noticed him until I was in the casino sitting at a slot machine and across the room there he stood. He was looking from side to side, back and forth trying to spot me. Immediately, without being noticed I told Mr. Money Bags, "We need to leave!" Mr. Money Bags was charming, somewhat cocky, much older, and paid like a slot machine for what he wanted. I gave him no explanation and jumped up and out of the casino we went! I left more as a result of the unexpected than fear, but considering Mr. Athlete had followed us so far, I didn't know what to expect. He didn't have the right, but I told him that the moment I was made aware he had been stalking me for five months.

My children, close friends, and co-workers were concerned for my life and I was concerned for his, because I would not live in a world of fear any longer! The final straw was on the day, the Angry One decided he would go home for his lunch break instead of his usual eating at his job. The Angry One was hot tempered, outgoing, and depending on the circumstances; ready to fight at the drop of a hat. He unexpectedly walked in and found Mr. Athlete in our home and asked him, "What are you doing here?" Mr. Athlete gave him some lame excuse that immediately led him to call me at my job. He said, "Mom, Mr. Athlete was walking down the hallway with some of your clothes over his arm and then left." I was livid and told the Angry One that I was headed home and I informed him that Mr. Athlete had no business being in our home and questioned how he was able to get in. Mr. Athlete was just another man who had lived up to what I believed all of them would; disappointment! Why had I trusted him when I took my key back to not have made a duplicate? Who knew how many times this man had been in our home before this moment considering we had parted ways several months earlier?

I left work and as I drove homeward bound, I dialed 911 and made the authorities aware of the situation I might have been walking into. Although, I was told he had left, yet I didn't know if he would return or not. As I began explaining the situation to the operator she asked, "Has he been violent towards you?" I answered, "No!" She then told me, "If he doesn't have any history of violence towards you, there is nothing we can do." I asked, "Do you understand what I have been telling you? He has been stalking me for months! Violent or not, this is not normal behavior and you're telling me you can't do anything about it?" She then instructed me to not go home. She was telling me not go to my own home where I had finally obtained my independence! She couldn't be serious; but she was! I told her, "There is no need for law enforcement for I will take care of this matter myself!" She warned me, "Ma'am, this conversation is being recorded and you're tone is threatening!" What nerve! She was concerned about me threatening him, but not him stalking me! As I continued driving to my home, entered the front entrance, turned the corner to park my vehicle, and proceeded to step out, immediately behind me was a law enforcement officer on his intercom demanding me to put my hands in the air!!

Things appeared to not be in my favor, but after I explained the situation to the officer, his reaction became one of the same concerns as others in regards to my safety. This concern was not shared by me for I was angry and felt that he had violated me! I had enough of being violated to last a lifetime and it was going to be him or me! I continued speaking with the officer and provided him with the necessary information he requested. After the official finally understood my position, it didn't take long before Mr. Athlete received warning from one conversation with a detective, and he was gone! Mr. Athlete was out and Mr. Money Bags was in; for the moment any way. Well, it wasn't as though he wasn't already in, because we had been conversing and meeting for months. It was easy for me to play the innocent role, but I had given Mr. Athlete reasons to feel insecure, yet it didn't justify his behavior. Mr. Money Bags didn't have any problems with giving his money to me to get what he wanted, and I didn't have any problems taking it. He had his reasons for all the lavishing and attention poured upon me because he wanted a trophy to display around his friends and brag about his younger girl toy. He was much older than me but was gracefully aged, but still couldn't satisfy me the way I needed to be; monetary or otherwise.

I was playing the part as though I was in a soap opera, and the money and perks kept coming. Although we felt we shared feelings for one another, neither of us were committed to our spouses, how could we be committed to each other? I was thirty five years old and still clueless as to what I wanted in a relationship, but no one could have told me that! My Mama had been deceased for less than a year and I was still embattled with pain and confusion! The realization of life was becoming a beautiful thing, regardless to if I understood it or not. He was seeing other women and I was doing what I wanted to do, yet still had the desire to be in a relationship that was about more than just the money! More so, I had begun to recognize that I was simply going through the motions. We connected on many levels but not the ones that were important. He began to turn me off completely when he decided he would tell me, "No man is going to be as good to you as me." I started to think in my mind, "Who in the hell does he think he was and who told him that he was all that? He didn't know me or the baggage I carried so this was the absolute out for me! I thought I was taking his feelings into consideration by trying to ease my way out, but then it was all about me! It was over in no time, another year had passed and my mind was focused on being alone. No relationship, no drama, no rules, no lying, no excuses, and no explanations! I had no concerns or cares other than those I always had; my children.

CHAPTER 9

The Effects on the Next Generation

Throughout this journey of my life and upon the birth of my eldest child through the birth of my youngest, my actions had affected them in ways I hadn't really been able to understand until now. My children had been in the midst of this turmoil, despite my many efforts to live a double life for years. It is very important as a parent and grandparent that I acknowledge the recognition of my past behavior, for as hard as I attempted to shelter them from my world of confusion and madness; they were engulfed in it through me! Through my anger, pain, abuse, fears, and heartache I had placed within them some of the very behavior that I had fought their entire lives to keep out!

My eldest often angry child and I were once very close in his younger years. He was considered a Mama's boy by those around us, but he simply enjoyed being in my company. I was seventeen years old when I birthed him, therefore enabling me to do things with him that older parents were limited to doing; like playing football, dodge ball, video games, etc. We loved spending time with each other and when we were together; my world was filled with happiness. As a young child, he was protective of me because although I didn't talk about many of the horrors of my past; he sensed them. Eventually, that sense was heightened when I would have to work or hustle for our survival and he would be left to care for his younger siblings. He was young and because of what many told him, didn't realize or understand that it was an avenue for me to provide for them; instead he understood it to be me running the streets having fun, or placing myself in harm's way. I chose to move to a community that was above my financial means, but I wanted the best life and education for my children that I could offer as a young parent. However, I placed him in the position of the parent over the child much too often, just as regrettably I see him doing today with his eldest child. I see his anger and frustration with me trying to tell him the right things to do, because he sometimes struggles with getting beyond the Mama of yesteryears. He holds on so tight to that person, that place, and that behavior because he now resides there. Although, he knows I'm right, he doesn't like hearing me tell him, "That's not who you are, you're better than that!" He simply says, "Mama, you use to do it!"

He fights so hard at being the best Dad that he can be to his children, but is repeating some of the same dreadful mistakes I did. He saw more than he should have, despite the fact that I disciplined them with an iron fist. I was more so harder on him because I used him being the oldest as an excuse for him taking care of my responsibilities. He appreciated the discipline and has told me so, but feels as though I try to dominate him as a man today. He wants to be a man, but I see what he can't; just as my Mother saw with me. I sometimes felt with her the same way he sometimes feels with me, and now realize that too often I made every excuse to justify my actions, when there was no justification! I refused to take on that accountability, despite the fact that it belonged to me. He is always packing my past on his shoulder, and recently I made a decision that placed him to believe that I put someone else before him. Despite the innocence of the person he says, "I understand Mama, but . . ." Yet again, I realize there are going to always be outside influences that are a driving force in how we deal with one another, but the choice is still a personal one. In addition, he too has and does things for all the wrong reasons and so the cycle continues, but it doesn't have to. He has chosen to pack so much although he knows he can talk to me about anything, he must come in truth; I have lived with what lies and secrets do, therefore can no longer accept them!

He will never admit the depth of the resentment he has towards his Donor Dad and takes tremendous offence when I tell him, "You need to deal with it in truth." He's changed in many ways from the young man I once knew, and I have to take some accountability for that, but he too has choices to make; we all do. He has a kind and loving heart, but it's often tugged in to places of confusion that I've lived and understand. I've beaten myself up for far too long until I began to reflect; "Son, I understand, I really do understand." I will no longer allow anyone to keep reminding me of who I was, and not who I am! He has begun talking with me more as a result of the change the Lord has made in my life. He's seen it more so than anyone else in my entire life. He's been there through times when no one else knew how difficult the pain really was. I'm also thankful that he has never been disrespectful towards me, but that was something that I absolutely raised them to not accept on any level, despite my flaws. I pray for him constantly and pray that upon reading this book he will honestly open the issues of his heart with God that he too might be set free!

My middle emotionally driven child has always been very close to me. Even when I do or did things that upset her, she still wanted to be around me. She can be clingy, but I enjoy every second of her company as much as she enjoys mine. Her memories differ from that of her siblings, although she too knows how diligent I am at making certain they are manner able and respectful young people. I constantly speak God's Word to her for it concerns me that they know where their strength truly comes from. I talk with her about my demise and what I would want her to do, but she cuts me off or begins to cry. She heartbreakingly says, "I can't imagine losing Daddy or you, I don't know what I would do." I tell her, "God will provide you with what you need, just as He has for me." This is a very touchy subject for her, but one that I need to talk about to prevent the same unknown that happened with me upon the death of my Mother. All the things that my Mama didn't do with me, I went totally overboard with doing with her. I did not allow her to sit on any man's lap other than her Father's, and sheltered her in many ways that have enabled some to take advantage of her kindness.

One of the most difficult tasks in the upbringing of my daughter was the fear of her going through the horror of sexual abuse. I have no doubt that I would have killed without hesitation, for I know what that pain had done to me! I took my children with me everywhere other than work or hustling and despite the woes of my madness; she is a compassionate, giving, and caring young woman. She desires to be in a healthy relationship as well, but often makes herself unreachable to young men that show an interest in her. She was in her first serious relationship at twenty one years old where she was manipulated and struggles with opening herself to another, but as long as she waits on the Lord, everything will work in her favor. She too has ways like me, but she's not a fighter! She's emotionally driven and I don't like to see weakness in her or any woman for that matter, because it sets up the foundation that can lead to disappointment every time! She can also make decisions about her life without thought, and get upset when things don't go as she desires them to. How could I make her understand something that she watched me struggle with for years? I can tell her because God made a way for me; even when I couldn't see. Her siblings tell her often, "You act just like Mama!" They sometimes say it as though it's an insult, but she accepts it with her head held high because she understands more, because we talk more. When she cries; I cry, when she laughs; I laugh, and when she hurts; I hurt! These feelings are not limited to her, but have often given the false impression that they are. She is my only living daughter and I want the best for her, but I now understand that will be determined by her and the choices she makes! "Learn from my mistakes and open your heart and mind to listen to that voice inside that comes from God that will lead you to all your heart's desires."

My youngest embattled child is the hard-worker in the bunch, and possesses the same work ethics as his Father. He is loyal to his family and friends even when that same loyalty may not be given in return! At two years old he drowned in a swimming pool and was pronounced dead at the scene, but the Lord spared his life and I tell him often, "You were born for greatness!" He recognizes and uses his gift to play basketball, but often struggles with the doubts that the enemy places within his heart and mind. We live in a society that is full of confusion and our children are falling into the traps every second; mine are not the exception. He was the most difficult to get through school because it his attention span was short and the teachers had to keep class interesting and challenging to keep his interest. The doctors wanted me to consider putting him on medication to calm him down, but I used the most effective tool; Spike, my personal leather assistant. When he was two months from graduating high school, we had a verbal exchange about him complaining about washing the dishes and he tried me! I put him out of our house and that was one of the hardest things I've ever had to do, but I could not allow him to make me go back on everything I had raised them on. He's big hearted and will give you his last without thought, or a reminder of his deed. If he can do; he does, and if he can't; he still tries.

He can be the most loving and thoughtful young man you could ever meet, and then he can be off the rector scale without warning! He's not one to impress people with materialistic items, although he enjoys them, but he is still going to bargain shop; that he learned from me. He doesn't have to iron every piece of clothing like I did for them as children, yet still feels comfortable just the way he is. He has confidence, but can sometimes be equally insecure. He has set high goals for himself and sometimes I believe his anger is being reflected through the fact that those goals have not yet been achieved. He is the most patient, but he definitely didn't learn that from me, yet the Lord continues to bless me to progress in that area daily. He doesn't talk much of my past nor uses it to make me feel guilty, but understands I was young and did the best I could; which wasn't too bad considering. He has deep compassion for me, but when I'm ill finds it's difficult to see me. He hides his emotion deep within and that often concerns me because I know the long term detriment of hidden pain. I don't see him as often as I once did, but he will take the time to send me a friendly reminder through a text message saying, "I love you special lady." They always come through when I least expect them, but God does work in mysterious ways. "Hammer, God has great things in store for your future, if you only put your trust in Him." The vicious cycle of dysfunction in our families doesn't have to continue if we take our positions and accountability within our families and our lives. We must step up to the plate for the sake of the generations to follow. Yes, we must!

CHAPTER 10

Lost and Found

I t was my children, the hustle, and I was moving forward with my life. The children were teenagers and close to graduating high school and certainly ready to get away from my household rules. My eldest child had graduated; my middle child was graduating in a couple of years, and my youngest child one year later. All these plans I had made once the children were gone, but was I really that excited about being on my own and all alone? As my usual routine continued, I was back to the joints when I wanted, hustling, or just out to have some fun with the fellas; minus the stress and mess. I had once again moved back to that place of familiarity that I knew wasn't a good place to be, yet there I was. Then along came my soul mate that made no impression on me upon our initial meeting. I had not a clue of the impact God predestined for him to be in my life!

I had been home after leaving from a Sunday morning worship service and was asked by a friend to come out to a pool tournament later to see many of the old hustle crew and others that would be there. It was being held at one of my favorite night spots and at first I was undecided if I was going or not. I was becoming bored with the same old environment, but boredom settled in, and my mind was quickly changed. As I entered, there were several local teams, as well as others from out of town and as I walked into the crowded joint, I found many familiar faces as well as, faces that I did not recognize. I was then asked by one of the regulars, "Sunshine, come over and sit at our table." Sunshine was a nickname that had been given to me many years prior by a close and dear friend. The rest of the place was packed as though we were at a Frankie Beverly and Maze concert. I accepted and began conversing with many around the table I knew; except one man. He had on a torn, dirty shirt, blue jean shorts, and some muddy boots! He looked like he had just come from a construction job pouring cement. I later discovered he owned horses and went to feed them after getting home from work every day and he too had been pulled in against his better judgment. As our various conversations continued, Mr. T asked, "What would you like to drink?" I arrogantly answered, "I don't drink!" He had no reaction to my abrasive response and delivered my drink of preference; The Real Thing and sat it down in front of me. I said, "Did you hear me say that I don't drink?" He calmly replied, "Ma'am, it was my turn to buy rounds for the table and since you're here, it would be disrespectful of me to exclude you." I had no response. As the hours passed, the table thinned out with the people that I knew and I found myself sitting at the table alone with Mr. T. It didn't take long before we began a very in-depth and interesting conversation of which I was shocked to discover we shared a lot in common.

We talked as though there was no one else in the building and I found the conversation appealing and stimulating, although I approached it with no expectation, just as it was apparent he was doing also. After we talked most of the night away, Mr. T walked me to my car and I gave him one of my business cards. Several days passed and he called to make me aware that he really enjoyed our previous day's conversation and would like to talk more often if possible. Although, I was not one for talking long over the phone, I found it a pleasant start to a new found friendship and we began conversing regularly. I usually rushed anyone off the phone because I liked to look people in their eyes when we talked about sincere and important matters for I had always been taught the eyes are the key to the soul. After many telephone conversations, we finally decided that we would meet each other for a movie and possibly some billiards afterwards. He knew how much I enjoyed shooting pool for it was the one thing that relaxed me and we discussed it often over the phone. The game took my mind off of many of the cares that seemed less important, and at the same time accommodated my competitiveness.

I could remain on the table until I just didn't want to shoot anymore, rather I won or lose. The time and date were set for the movie and this was only the third time I had seen Mr. T in person. As I prepared to meet him, I parked and almost immediately noticed something small that had a huge impact on me. In our many earlier conversations, I always reminded him of how precious time was and I didn't take it for granted. I was extremely time conscious and took offense when others weren't. As I parked in the parking lot of the theatre, Mr. T walked right beside my car without noticing me or it and headed straight towards our meeting destination in the front of the building. I got out of my car with many thoughts and raced to catch up with him and informed him that he had just passed right by me. He smiled with pleasure that I approved of his efforts to honor my time consideration and we proceeded into the theatre.

Afterwards, we went to a local family pool hall and shot billiards and I was shocked yet again, for he could shot the game! He was almost too good to be true and the longer I was in his company; the more I noticed qualities in him I liked. He didn't smoke or drink and was not putting on a performance for my enjoyment; it was who he was. This man impressed me with what many would consider to be the small things, but was big to me. I had not told him much outside of the things that in most cases should have chased him off full speed ahead! I made every attempt to bring this friendship to an end before it could develop into anything more. I didn't want to hurt anyone else due to my recklessness and didn't want to be hurt by anyone due to theirs. Shortly thereafter, I received word that my dear friend had passed away out of town and the news shook me to my core. She had left to care for her sick Mother and she was gone! I didn't want to go because I just knew I would not handle it well, but despite my fears I knew I had to be there to pay my final respect. She was a dependable friend who had my back through some of the roughest times in my life. She never judged me and frequently told me, "You can do anything!" She was always encouraging me and when my Mama died, she was there to offer her support and words of encouragement to me. I didn't even remember to call her, but she showed up ready to do whatever she could just as she had the ten years I had known her. She was just like me in many ways and that was one of the many things I loved about her. She said what she meant, meant what she said, and always kept it real! I respected her because I never had to worry about what she was thinking; she would tell me. Those types of people in my life were few and far between; they were an endangered species.

As I traveled the journey and arrived to meet one of her relatives, I tried to be the strength that she had asked of me; for we had discussed what to do upon the other's death many times. The time had drawn near and we were heading to her home going service and I was fighting with everything in me to keep it together. The service was uplifting just as she would have wanted and as it came to a close, I didn't go to view her remains and turned my back as they escorted her casket down the aisle of the church passed me. I then prepared to exit and to my astonishment, they had opened her casket in the church's corridor and I was caught totally off guard! Seeing her lay there motionless, a wig on her head, and witnessing what the cancer had done drained all the strength out of me. I began to run; running to nowhere, but just wanted this to not be true! As her daughter ran to get me, I was out of control! She was comforting me when I should have been comforting her! I finally pulled myself together and we loaded up for the processional to head to her final resting place in a nearby town. After our arrival, I had already made up my mind that I wouldn't go back for the repast; it was just too much for me. I explained to her children that I was not helping them and they understood. I was a basket case, yet got on the highway to head back home; alone! Alone on the highway, driving in zombie mode, and after three and a half hours or so my mobile phone rang; it was Mr. T.

He had offered to ride with me and I refused because I still had my guard up with him. He was checking to see where we were. However I had to tell him that my intended passenger never showed up, and so I headed up and down the highway by myself. This was no big deal to me for my stubbornness was often how most people saw me, but Mr. T was disturbed by it, because he knew how difficult that trip was for me. I didn't bother to explain why I had not informed him that I had taken out by myself and he didn't ask. He knew it would only create tension that I was not going to deal with! The longer I drove and we continued to talk, it was soothing to hear his genuine concern for me. This was new to me because most people in my life had dealt with me for what they could get out of me or other selfish reasons; just as I had dealt with most people. Why didn't I accept his offer to ride with me? Why couldn't I see that he really cared? He was just being the gentleman that he was by trying to make himself accessible to me when I needed someone to be there. Yet, I still refused to give in to the possibility of allowing him in and seeing me weak! As we continued to talk, the reality of this deep loss sank in deeper and deeper and I didn't want to be alone that night so I asked, "May I come by when I get back into the city?" He sympathetically without hesitation said, "Of course you can!"

I arrived at his home and he had already prepared me something to eat, and after I cleaned the plate I was fast asleep on his sofa. I awoke the following morning touching all over my body to see if my clothes were still on, called for him, began questioning him, and apologized for falling asleep on his sofa. He began to question my issues of distrust and assured me that he would not do anything to me that I didn't want him to, and then proceeded to the kitchen to cook breakfast for me. This was a time that I really needed someone who was sincere and he came through in a big way! As the weeks passed, he invited me over for dinner and I would go over to have him wait on me hand and foot. If he was a dream, I didn't want to be awakened!

CHAPTER 11

A New Beginning

We gradually entered into a new found relationship and although we were spending lots of time together, I was still waiting on the ball to drop. I took really ill and Mr. T had to rush me to the emergency room they me admitted due to the severity of my illness. He was at the hospital and stayed with me for hours on end to support me on every level. They were prepping me for test after test to try to find out what was going on with me. After being there for a couple of days, I had a male companion who I desired to come to see me. I didn't want Mr. T to know, so I sent him away on a lie by asking him if he would go to check on my children at home and stay there with them through the night. The following day my condition had not improved and they were simply giving me medication for comfort, but no diagnosis or results. As I laid there thinking, I knew that God was dealing with me, yet I still tried to justify my wrongs in my mind. The only justification for a lie is the truth! That night, Mr. T asked, "May I stay the night with you?" The question was easy to answer because I didn't want to be alone. I awakened in the middle of the night from a morphine drip, looked at the foot of the bed, saw him sleeping, and sitting up with his legs propped up on the bed in a straight back chair. The feeling that came over me was indescribable, but I felt the Lord opened my eyes to see something that I had missed over and over again!

I could not believe or understand why he chose to stay with everything I had said and done. I was so convicted by that revelation that I was compelled to confess my lie to him later in the morning.

When I told him what I had done he simply said, "I know." I didn't understand how he could possibly know for I was telling him for the first time. After being released from the hospital I returned home to return back to the hospital a few months later. This unknown illness was making me sicker and sicker and Mr. T was still by my side. As I traveled from hospital to hospital and doctor to doctor, I knew but continued to ignore that the Lord had a request of me; marry that man! He's the one, yet I was already married and although we had been separated for all those years, I was fearful of losing my security in the marriage. Mr. T and I discussed the possibility of marriage but I told him, "I've not ever been in a committed relationship." It never even crossed my mind what he thought about my reality, but it was important for me to be honest because he was deserving of the truth. My illness continued to take me in and out of the hospital, back and forth to the doctor, and each time the diagnosis was unknown or unexplainable. Shortly after, due to my illness and the absentees from my job, I resigned my position and moved into his house with my two children that were still home. After my third admission into the hospital in less than two years, I knew what I had to do! Once I was released and we arrived home, I walked Mr. T over to a calendar on our dining room table and said, "Pick the date!" The date he chose was three months from that day! I talked with Mr. Good Guy because I needed him to understand why the time had come for me to divorce him. I had already wasted so many years of our lives. I felt it only fair considering all I had put him through to ask, "Do you think that you and I can make this marriage work?" Upon his thought of that very profound question he answered saying, "No, I don't." I proceeded with the divorce and in May 2003 we were legally divorced.

It started off a little rough in the beginning because Mr. Good Guy had become just as comfortable in our dead end marriage as I had. Yet, in time we were able to go through the process and maintain a healthy friendship, despite our moments when we really had to fight through the pain and disappointment of why our marriage failed. We wanted our children to not have to deal with the after effects of our decision, yet know this would be beneficial for all parties involved. In February 2005, Mr. T and I married on a beautiful, rainy day where everything went exactly the way the Lord desired it to, even though there were those who attempted to sabotage me behind my back to my new husband. I had reached a point that it was no longer as shocking or surprising to me to hear people making me to be someone that I wasn't! Despite the rain outside, the sun was shining brightly inside! I had married the man who the Lord chose for me; finally! As we adjusted to our new marriage, we did lots of talking for we both had baggage from our previous marriages that we did not want to affect our current one. This was a huge task for me because it was difficult to trust and although we were married the old baggage was still there. We started by making decisions in regards to how we would overcome many of the hardships that had destroyed our previous unions. This was new territory for me because I was a talker and needed to be a listener, but he balanced me. Many had thrown the towel in on our marriage before it ever started, but they were not the ones who had put the union together; God had!

A few years later, I was notified by a family member that the Beast had died and his funeral was quickly approaching. I had mixed emotions that required I seek some spiritual counseling to assist in deciding if I should go or not. After I talked, prayed, and took much consideration in facing this demon, I decided to go with Mr. T and Scary Little Boy in tow. As we traveled the highway, I was a child all over again and my insecurities, doubts, and fears questioned if I had made the right decision! After we arrived, we prepared to enter the funeral home and I began to feel my palms getting sweaty and my heart rate increased with each step. The little girl in me was screaming on my inside with agony from the torment of having been victimized by this devil over and over again, and I was here to look in his evil face again! As we slowly approached his casket, Mr. T was stroking my hand and softly telling me, "Stay calm, you can do this." I had prayed the entire journey, for I knew I was struggling pertaining to this necessary but extremely difficult chapter closure in my life. As we drew closer and closer, I could see his bald head, and just the sight sent chills through my entire body! All those feelings inside of me came rushing like a raging wind! Mr. T continued caressing my hand, standing in front of me, coaching me to just look and move, but I stood there and stared at him! I stared into the face of that monster as I had never done before! He looked exactly as I remembered and had not changed one bit! I was looking evil in the face for the final time or was I? His face and the pain were sketched in my memory forever!

He had taken my innocence from me as though I were nothing and I just wanted to lean over, shake him, scream at him, spit in his face and leave! Mr. T pulled me away as though he could read my every thought. As we went to our seats for the service and it reached time for expressions; once again it was taking all I had to keep my seat!

I was thinking, "Get up and say something, tell them what he did to you so many years ago, tell them the pain and heartache you had suffered as a result of his filthiness!" Once again Mr. T began caressing my hand and then out of nowhere, the Scary Little Boy jumped up to walk to the front of the chapel and expressed his words about The Beast! He began to say, "I respected him and he gave me good advice." He didn't have one bad thing to say about this evil man; not one thing! I was in utter shock as I attempted to understand where all his words were coming from! My mind was racing, "Who is he talking about?" These feelings worsened with each tear that dropped from his eyes as he continued to speak. How could he shed tears for this monster and why didn't I tell him? Why didn't I tell him the truth? Why didn't I tell anyone? After the service, came to a close and we went to the cemetery, I was relieved it was over! The Beast was dead and I must move on with my life and stop allowing this pain to continue to devour me! After we returned home, I continued to go back and forth with my emotions and to the joints doing what I had known for so long. Mr. T was home and not pleased with my decision making, but continued to tell me, "I'm praying for you." As I entered the joint, I greeted all the regular patrons, headed to the table with my pool stick in tow, and turned back to the bar to order my favorite soft drink. As I stood at the bar waiting on the house lady to bring my drink, I heard a soft voice ask me, "What are you doing here? I began to look around for I had been asked that question many times before, but this time no one was there. I sat on the bar stool filled with confusion, yet once again the voice asked the same question.

As I sat there thinking to myself, in a daze, and embattled within, I could not answer the question! I stood up, returned to the table where I laid my pool stick case, closed the case, gave my love, and outta there I went! I did not leave out of fear, because the voice was soft and calm, but I recognized that God had spoken to my heart and I could not ignore it any longer. I had heard the voice before but something made this time different? I couldn't grasp why I had ignored it the previous times, but where did I go from here? There had been so many questions I had no answers for, but in the process I finally was ready to surrender! I was already so tired, weary, and had spent so many years not really knowing which side of the fence I wanted to stand on. The Lord was blessing me, but I was still doing the same foolish things I had done since I began spiraling out of control at thirteen years old! I was actively participating in my church, holding many positions, and encouraging others with a façade of who I wanted them to believe I was. I was living a lie! I was doing all the right things when I was there, but living any kind of way when I wasn't; God knew! God knew what my heart desired and enabled me to get still long enough to receive what He had for me. I wanted to serve Him in truth and stop wearing the many masks that had become worn through the years! I left knowing it was healing time for me on many levels. I left knowing I had to let go of the chains that had kept me in bondage for so many years. I left knowing I had to stop allowing the challenges of the past to be the determining factor for my present and my future.

I left the joints for the last time at thirty nine years of age and was finally starting a new beginning!

CHAPTER 12

Reflections

As I reflect over many of the writings in this book, so much is still left unsaid, but I know God has much more in store for me. The journey to this place has not been an easy one, but I know today that God was with me all the time. Although, I was blinded by what I thought to be, the Lord has opened my eyes to see His divine plan for my life. He opened this path for me to release truth into existence for the sake of us all. I'm willing to run this race until the end and can no longer continue to allow the pains of the past to prevent me from taking my life back! I have been challenged from the very beginning with health, family, friends, church members, and anything the devil thought he could use to keep me from pressing forward. There have been so many times in my life when I know I should have and could have died, but God kept me for this moment in time, and He's not through with me yet. I often wondered why many of the trials and tribulations of this life didn't achieve what the devil intended them to, but I now know that it was because God had other plans for my life. I wanted to be set free so long ago, but didn't have the first clue as to how to reach that place. It was a lonesome highway to travel when it seemed there was only one way to go. I was convinced that because of my wrongdoings I was unworthy of any blessings that the Lord had for me. I allowed the devil to convince me through others and my own foolish thoughts that I was going to fail at anything I attempted.

From a ripe young age, I believed everything was my fault and became consumed with shame, guilt, and pain, but I now understand it was the journey I had to travel to recognize the calling that had been placed on my life many years ago. There were many times that I could have altered that journey, but my stubbornness and rebellion caused me to travel many roads that led to dead ends. This is not a woman's story; this is a life's story! My being a woman has nothing to do with repeating the same disastrous mistakes over and over again; mistakes are not about gender. I wasn't having fun out there anymore and hadn't been for some time, yet I kept going! The world offered me no relief and what I thought I was seeking was never to be found in this sin filled world! It wasn't because of my family, friends, acquaintances, situations, circumstances or anything else; it was me! I had been surrounded all my life by people who disappointed me over and over again, yet I still had to take accountability for my own actions.

I have learned that it's so much easier to play the blame game, because then I could look at everyone else's flaws and not look at my own. I knew I didn't want that life any longer, yet it was tough for me because I thought I needed the acceptance the streets had given me. It was time for me to do what I should have been doing long ago, because this journey had enabled me to help others in many ways. God set my life on course and I took it off course, but thank the Lord for allowing me the opportunity to be used for His service through this forum and any others that He opens for me. We go through life to learn from our mistakes, not to continue making them as if we're going to live forever. I was fortunate on many levels in the streets for often I was placed in harm's way, but God protected me! Even when I was in the midst of my madness and thought I was unworthy to be kept: He kept me! The enemy would tempt me to go back out there through boredom and other vices, but God still gave me strength to say, "No, I'm not going." I will never forget where the Lord has brought me from, but I have no intentions of turning back.

Many times I cried because I didn't know if I had made the right decision and was battling harder and harder every single day! I would find myself intentional doing things to sabotage my own happiness and sometimes that of others, despite not wanting to. Living life in the past is like living in quick sand; the more we wiggle, the deeper we sink. I had been sinking fast and it was through my very own thoughts and behaviors that I no longer could accept! Even after I recognized what the Lord was doing in my life, the enemy still tried to convince me to do things that I knew I had been delivered from. Thank God for enabling me to recognize it for what it was. The devil comes to kill, steal, destroy, and doesn't want me or any of God's children to make it to Heaven, but the God I serve has made promises to me that I believe wholeheartedly! The devil is an illusionist, but I am a child of the King! I knew that I had been out in the world for far too long and now I desired something that had been placed in me as a child that was not evil! As I continued to ask the Lord for guidance, He began to show me things that could not be ignored. I grew up hearing it's my way or the highway, and I often said those very words to my own children, but I wasn't running anything! God has always been in control and therefore, I've stopped being the victim and instead the survivor! I can remember being one of the very people who said what I wouldn't and/or couldn't do because that was what I heard, but that is how the devil operates. He preys on our weaknesses to convince us that we're not worth anything because we were abused, misused, talked about, scorn, criticized, and any other negative thoughts that may be lingering in our finite minds.

I thank God for this journey and to share it with my readers and everyone whose paths I cross to know that no matter what man/woman have to say; God has the final word! He makes the eternal decision for our lives and does the choosing of those who desire to be used by Him. I've learned to not give in to the ways of the ones that desire to travel the path of destruction for I lived on it for too long. I know live for Christ that someone might see His wonderful works in me and desire to be set free! I thank God for saving me because He could have called my name in the midst of the battle between the darkness and the light. As you have read, this revelation did not come over night, but it came when I surrendered all to the Lord. I can't speak truth and not say I don't sometimes still struggle with the mysteries of the unknown, but I have made a conscious choice to follow the Lord. It is not a decision that I can make for anyone else other than me, although it is one of my greatest desires.

All the rejection, pain, agony, sorrow, and mischief that possibly could have been avoided, I now understand it was required for me to be a testimony for someone else. God created me for greatness and I was the only one getting in the way! I can no longer live a lie for the sake of pleasing others and allow my soul salvation to be at risk. I love regardless to if the love is returned or not, because God doesn't hold me accountable for how others treat me, He holds me accountable for how I treat them. The Lord directed me to this place within to free me from the anguish of living through life holding on to dead weight. I have forgiveness, love, peace, joy, and truth in my heart; finally! I made so many mistakes, but God knew I would and still loved me; He still loves me! It took me most of my life to surrender because this pain kept me imprisoned with shame, disgust, misery, guilt, and heartache, but it developed me into the new creature God is seeking in these last and evil days. Regardless of what may be said, this is important because I have the responsibility to do my part as His earthly vessel. All mentioned are my personal experiences and encounters; individually and collectively. I pray that by opening up my patched wounds, it will free us all from the shame, guilt, fear, doubts and heartache that continue to keeping us in bondage; often for a lifetime.

It is truth time and it has begun with me; it is the only way we can grow beyond the pain. No matter how painful this truth was to me, it was more important that it no longer be contained for the sake of us all! Sincere freedom comes through truth; so take the masks off and open your hearts to receive all the glorious blessings the Lord has! The Lord is true to His every promise and will show us all for who we really are. The time for us to get our lives in order with the Lord is right now! "I must work the works of him that sent me, while it is day: the night cometh, when no man can work. (St. John 9: 4) We serve a God that is merciful and loves us unconditionally; the least we can do is trust Him. "Trust in the Lord with all thine heart; and lean not unto thine own understanding. In all thy ways acknowledge him, and he shall direct thy paths." (Proverbs 3:5-6) I wanted to be free! I will be free**! I am free!**

My prayer: Lord, I thank you for opening the necessary doors to write this book and bless the many who will read my story and be set free from bondage through the Holy Spirit. Lord, I thank you for giving me the strength to speak the unspoken and I pray that it reaches those you desire and they be healed from whatever they may be going through in their lives. I thank you for freeing me through this truth and no matter the situation or circumstances; I thank you for not giving up on me. Lord, I trust you and know that you are with me all the time providing for me, protecting me, loving me, comforting me, and keeping me in your precious care. Lord, if I had ten thousand tongues I couldn't thank you enough for all you've done for me! Lord, I thank you! I thank you! I thank you and I praise your holy name! In the Mighty Name of Jesus! Amen!

"I press toward the mark for the prize of the high calling of God in Jesus Christ." Philippians 3:14

~Lord, I'm still pressing~

Amen!